Praise for *This I Know*

In uncertain times, it is imperative to be grounded in timeless truths, convinced of the un-changing nature of the one true God. *This I Know* is an anchor of hope to calm your fears and bolster your faith. Move from head knowledge to heart knowledge as you interact with this captivating and approachable study.

KATIE M. REID
Bible study facilitator and author of *Made Like Martha*

This I Know is for those who long for a secure future in the middle of an uncertain world. Laura Dingman has done a masterful job of helping her readers identify truths that transform fear into strong faith and purposeful action. Invite your friends to join you in an adventure that will take you into God's Word for answers while giving you an opportunity for extraordinary personal growth as you respond to the application questions. Don't miss this exceptional study!

CAROL KENT
Speaker and author of *He Holds My Hand: Experiencing God's Presence and Protection*

Having known Laura Dingman for more than two decades, I have watched her live out the very title of her book. What Laura has written will help her readers courageously let go of their security when it comes time for them to reach for their destiny.

GARY JOHNSON
Senior minister at Indian Creek Christian Church, Indianapolis, IN; author of *Leader Shift: Helpful Insights for a Go-Honoring Transition* and *Too Much: Living with Less in the Land of More*

How will we ever be able to let go of our own need for control until we know the Person who actually holds it all? Laura helps us, step by step, release our own control and anxiety while at the same time teaching us how to hold fast to Jesus.

JEN FERGUSON
Speaker and coauthor of *Pure Eyes, Clean Heart: A Couple's Journey to Freedom from Pornography*

What a powerful, beautifully composed Bible study that invites readers to know Jesus as our steady cornerstone who loves us more than we can imagine! This study truly helps us fix our eyes on Jesus and know Him deeply as we examine key Scriptures in life-changing ways.

HEATHER HOLLEMAN
Speaker, teacher, and author of *Seated with Christ*, *Guarded by Christ*, and *Included in Christ*

Laura's writing is as accessible as it is transformative, sweeping up readers with simplicity and changing them with profundity. If you find yourself cowering in fear, sprinting from uncertainty, or drowning in worry, *This I Know* was written for you. Breathe in its wisdom, and exhale your anxieties.

JONATHAN MERRITT
Author of *Learning to Speak God from Scratch*; contributing writer for the *Atlantic*

Infusing truth with real-life experiences, Laura reminds us how we are loved in the midst of mess, we are cared for when things feel hopeless, and that the pain will always be used to make something more beautiful for God. This book will encourage you no matter where your fear and worry want to take you.

MARY GRAHAM
Blogger at trustychucks.com and writer for the *Huffington Post*

Studying God's Word through *This I Know* allowed my soul to exhale! Remember what you already know about who God is and His great love toward you, while also reaching out to grasp new truths. In the process, you'll let go of the anxiety and fear holding you back from being who you were created to be.

CHERIE LOWE
Author of *Slaying the Debt Dragon: How One Family Conquered Their Money Monster and Found an Inspired Happily Ever After*

This I Know is a guidebook of unchangeable truths about God and His Word that will provide comfort to one's soul. Practical yet inspirational—for those looking for a Bible study that teaches how to find a life of greater peace in the presence of God, this is for you.

NANCY J. KANE
Conference speaker, author of *From Fear to Love*; associate professor, Moody Bible Institute

Laura Dingman's first study, *I Am Found,* was a game changer of shame release for me. This new study will take the reader on an incredible journey of trust in the unchanging character and goodness of God in the midst of a changing world.

JENNIFER HAND
Executive director of Coming Alive Ministries; author of *Confessions of a Coffee Cup Collector*

this i KNOW

TRUSTING YOUR UNKNOWN FUTURE TO A KNOWN GOD

LAURA DINGMAN

MOODY PUBLISHERS

CHICAGO

Unless otherwise indicated, Scripture quotations are taken from the Holy Bible, New International Version®, NIV®. Copyright © 1973, 1978, 1984, 2011 by Biblica, Inc.™ Used by permission of Zondervan. All rights reserved worldwide. www.zondervan.com. The "NIV" and "New International Version" are trademarks registered in the United States Patent and Trademark Office by Biblica, Inc.™

Scripture quotations marked NLT are taken from the Holy Bible, New Living Translation, copyright ©1996, 2004, 2007, 2013, 2015 by Tyndale House Foundation. Used by permission of Tyndale House Publishers, Inc., Carol Stream, Illinois 60188. All rights reserved.

Scripture quotations marked NASB are from the New American Standard Bible®, Copyright © 1960, 1962, 1963, 1968, 1971, 1972, 1973, 1975, 1977, 1995 by The Lockman Foundation. Used by permission. (www.Lockman.org)

Scripture quotations marked The Message are taken from *The Message*, copyright © 1993, 1994, 1995, 1996, 2000, 2001, 2002 by Eugene H. Peterson. Used by permission of NavPress. All rights reserved. Represented by Tyndale House Publishers, Inc.

Emphasis to Scripture has been added by the author.

Edited by Pam Pugh
Cover design: Dean Renninger
Cover image of rocks copyright © 2017 by Andrea Danti / Shutterstock (536548897). All rights reserved.
Cover image of watercolor © 2015 by Gerd Altmann / Pixabay (1076264). All rights reserved.
Author photo: Kaitlyn Huff
Interior design: Erik M. Peterson

Library of Congress Cataloging-in-Publication Data

Names: Dingman, Laura, author.
Title: This I know : trusting your unknown future to a known God / Laura
   Dingman.
Description: Chicago : Moody Publishers, 2018.
Identifiers: LCCN 2017040144 (print) | LCCN 2017047171 (ebook) | ISBN
   9780802495846 | ISBN 9780802415967
Subjects: LCSH: Trust in God--Christianity--Textbooks. | Providence and
   government of God--Christianity--Textbooks. | Christian women--Religious
   life.
Classification: LCC BV4637 (ebook) | LCC BV4637 .D45 2018 (print) | DDC
   231--dc23
LC record available at https://lccn.loc.gov/2017040144

ISBN: 978-0-8024-1596-7

We hope you enjoy this book from Moody Publishers. Our goal is to provide high-quality, thought-provoking books and products that connect truth to your real needs and challenges. For more information on other books and products written and produced from a biblical perspective, go to www.moodypublishers.com or write to:

Moody Publishers
820 N. LaSalle Boulevard
Chicago, IL 60610

1 3 5 7 9 10 8 6 4 2

Printed in the United States of America

To Matt—my favorite companion into the unknown.
You have taught me to see the hand of God in the hard things.
I wouldn't trade our story for anything.

CONTENTS

ABOUT THE COVER

Throughout the Scriptures, God asked the Israelites to gather rocks to build altars of remembrance. These stacked stones would serve as guideposts for not only those who gathered them, but for future generations as well. Whenever someone asked what the stones meant, Israel recounted the story of God's miracles among them.

Years later, these stacked stones are known as *cairns,* a Scottish-Gaelic word. These cairns serve as landmarks on trails for travelers. They're used now to help sojourners find their way home.

A NOTE FROM THE AUTHOR

In our chaotic culture, worry and anxiety measure at an all-time high. So much of what swirls around us is out of our control. Plans failed. Dreams shattered. Relationships broken. Events in the news concern us. Everyday life isn't so ordinary anymore. Optimism fades and fear flourishes.

Through it all, we long for hope. We long for freedom from the uninvited, worrisome thoughts that take over. We want something different, something else, *something more holy*. But how do we find it when our circumstances are challenging and we don't know what may come?

When so much is unknown, we need to refocus on what is known—about our God and His Word. We are desperate for God to anchor our present even though we don't know what the future holds. *This I Know* is a six-week Bible study that walks through biblical truths you can clutch tightly in the unknown. These truths find their roots in the trustworthy characteristics of God.

Everyone wonders what his or her future holds. At different times in our lives, anxiety and worry grip our reality in the present. God longs for us to have a worry-free (not a pain-free) life void of anxiety and fear. *This I Know* helps us learn more about the God who has made Himself known in the printed pages of His Word. When we know and experience God, our unknown future doesn't look so daunting. And that's the kind of peace everyone craves.

I am praying for you as you walk through these pages. I don't know what lies ahead for you, but I know the God who does know. And He goes before you in all of it and is with you every step of the way.

INTO THE UNKNOWN
AN INTRODUCTION TO THIS STUDY

The year is 1985. Marty McFly discovers that his scientist friend, Doc Brown, built an epic machine for time travel from a customized DeLorean. In this car fueled by plutonium pilfered from terrorists, Marty, desperate to escape the bad guys, travels back to 1955. At first the adventure seems harmless, fun even, but his presence in 1955 changes the course of his and others' lives. He alters his future by going back to the past. Can't be all bad, right?

Sometimes I'd like the ability to hitch a ride in the time-hopping DeLorean so I could change some choices in the past to effect a better future. I'd also use that DeLorean to travel into the future so I could experience *right now* what is to come. I have a deep desire to know what's coming. And what's not. Perhaps if I knew, I'd have a greater sense of security, giving me the confidence I need to step into whatever blurry season is next.

On the other hand, I'm certain if I had seen ahead of time some of the trials I've lived through, I would have just plain quit. Given up altogether.

We all desire to be in control, don't we? I know I do. I want to see what's coming, but really only in an effort to somehow control events and to somehow avoid problems. To secure joy and good fortune as if I can create a life free from suffering for myself and those I love.

But the stark truth is that seeing the future isn't possible. We know this reality, but it doesn't keep us from trying, does it? We cannot control what will come. We cannot sidestep struggle. Sure, our choices can determine the trajectory of things at times, but there is no guarantee for any of it.

Our future is unknown.

Several months ago, I was praying through some big obstacles in my life, wondering what was coming. Change whirled around me at a rate I couldn't control. It all seemed so insurmountable, looming in front of me. My anxiety reeled. I begged God to show me something. *Anything.* I wrote phrase after phrase in my journal listing all the things I just didn't know as I pleaded for some answers.

Then I sensed the Holy Spirit whispering, "I know you don't know what's ahead. So, tell Me what you *do* know."

What *do* I know?

I thought about it for a moment and began to write, "Wherever we go, *this* I know . . ." A list of things I know—without a doubt—about our God poured over the pages of my journal. Things I had come to know by repeatedly experiencing them. Things proven true.

You love me. So much. You see me and know how You put me together for the road ahead and behind and right now. For the first time in my life, I know this and I am grateful.

You have a plan and the plan is good. I trust You, Jesus. I know this and I am grateful.

You are good. Always. I know this and I am grateful.

You are for me. You fight for me when I can't fight for myself. I know this and I am grateful.

You never change. You are constant, unwavering, loyal, faithful. I know this and I am grateful.

You are redeeming and restoring everything. I know this and I am grateful.

You will lead me. I will hear Your voice telling me which way to go. I know this and I am grateful.[1]

1. This is an excerpt from my personal journal dated November 19, 2015.

Corrie ten Boom once said, "Never be afraid to trust your unknown future to a known God."

Our God made Himself known. He is found in the pages of Scripture. He reveals Himself in creation. He allows us to experience His essence through life in community. He shows up and shows Himself quite regularly if only we pay enough attention.

While He certainly isn't explainable, He has made Himself known.

When we fix our eyes on Jesus, the author and perfecter of our faith, instead of on our unknown future, worry dissipates. Anxiety melts. Hope solidifies. Faith grows. *Life changes.*

Of course, times of pain and fear and suffering still come, but what we do with it—in the midst of it—is different because *we are different.* Because our view of God is different. I don't know where you are or what lies ahead for you. I don't know what kind of scattered pieces you're trying to put back together. I don't know what form your worries and anxieties are taking these days. But this I know: God will *never* leave you or forsake you (Heb. 13:5). Ever.

USING THIS STUDY

We will walk through Bible passages beginning with Paul's address to the men of Athens concerning the God who is known. We continue through truths of God's nature of abundance and not of scarcity and Jesus as the cornerstone who holds all things together. As we journey through the story of Jehoshaphat in 2 Chronicles 20 and through passages like James 1, Habakkuk 3, and Psalm 46, we will recognize God's goodness in trials that either have come or will come in the future. To wrap up, we will learn the power that remembering holds for us from the story of Joshua 3.

Each week begins with an introduction outlining a major truth about knowing God. It's important to have this overview as a reference for everything else you'll encounter, as it will serve as a backdrop for the daily time you will spend at the feet of Jesus.

Following the introduction are five daily lessons unpacking statements about who God is. These begin with some thoughts connecting them to the overview in the introduction. These devotional thoughts will guide you as you spend time at the feet of Jesus, asking Him to faithfully impart wisdom, gently unveil weaknesses, and boldly proclaim promises you need to know in His Word. He is ready to do that if only we will set aside the time and ask Him.

You will be dwelling in the Scriptures throughout this study. Some of the methods may be new to you and some you may be so familiar with that you are tempted to rush through them. Take your time. Savor the passages. Instead of just reading the Scripture, let the Scripture read you. Allow the Holy Spirit to do His work; let the truth He reveals sink in.

Some of the Scripture texts are printed for you in the study. Others you will be invited to read in your own Bible. You'll be encouraged to mark words or phrases that matter to you in the moment. If you're not comfortable writing in your Bible, use this study book or a journal. You can also print out the passages from biblegateway.com and mark those sheets.

Following the devotional thoughts and Scripture reading, you'll see a suggested prayer for the day. These words are just starters for your own prayers. He longs to hear your words as well, so after reading the prayer for the day, pray your own prayer. Prayer is simply conversing with God. Be honest. Tell Him what you are thinking and feeling—even if it's hard. Ask for what you desire and confess your need for Him to do His work in your life.

The last segment each day is a short journaling prompt to help you process what you've read and discovered. Journaling is a go-to discipline for me. Over the years, I have filled journals and am amazed by what God has shown me through writing to Him. On the pages of my journal I ask my deepest questions. I honestly hash out my feelings. And I wait for His response. It's a beautiful dance and I'm hoping you'll find a little bit of the dance joyful.

The prompts are similar each day, but the message and your insights will change. Your own questions will be different. Writing out your thoughts and feelings is a simple practice that will record your journey, allowing you to look back and see tangible evidence of how God moved in this season of your life—an important part of learning and living out new truths.

IMPORTANT TO NOTE

Over the next several weeks we will be talking about anxiety and worry. Anxiety manifests itself in many ways, and fear fuels different responses: there is the downward spiral kind of anxiety, but there is also medically diagnosed anxiety. I have experienced both.

We are not referring to the medically diagnosed types of anxiety in this study, nor should anything here replace needed medical care. I have been a recipient of medication for anxiety and depression. I've also dealt with anxiety that resulted from a poorly managed thought life and out-of-control feelings with their roots in lies. I've seen both aspects of anxiety and there is a difference between them.

Sometimes in church circles, people will say your anxiety and your depression will disappear if you pray more or spend more time in the Word or if you just trust God more. While these are wonderful disciplines and can lift a person's spirits, sometimes medical intervention is necessary to alleviate anxiety and depression.[2]

KEEP GOING

As we journey together through this study, we will learn to take every thought captive and make it obedient to Christ (2 Cor. 10:5). Embracing new truths will lead us to do this. I invite you to dig into the truths for each day.

When you've committed to set aside time each day to change the way you think and orient yourself toward Jesus and His Word, the enemy will do his very best to

2. If you discover along the way that you need to speak to someone, please be courageous and seek the counsel of a trusted medical or psychiatric professional. Please know there is no shame in doing so. Our mental and emotional health is just as important as our spiritual and physical health. You might also check out http://www.aacc.net/resources/find-a-counselor/.

ruin your resolve. You will have obstacles. You'll probably miss days and feel like you've failed.

Whatever you do, don't quit. That's exactly what the enemy wants. And here's why: when you begin to believe these truths about who God is, your life *will* be different. The enemy will no longer be able to shackle you with worry and fear. Anxiety will not sit in the driver's seat anymore. God will be driving and the enemy will do anything to stop that from happening.

So dig in. Dig into the Scriptures to see what they say about this God we long to know. Dig into your own soul asking Jesus to grow your faith and trust in Him. Dig into your thinking to uproot any patterns contrary to the Word of God, asking the Holy Spirit to retrain your brain and create new ways of thought that align your thinking with the truth.

REFLECTION

We are a society void of reflection these days. Socrates once said, "The unexamined life is not worth living." I agree that our lives seem more worth living when we stop and reflect on what God is up to, examining our life and what He's doing in us. So the end of each week is designed for you to reflect on what you've learned over the previous five days. The truths we've encountered will be listed for you to review. Ask yourself these questions: Is there a theme in what God is showing me? What action steps do I need to follow for this new thing God is doing in me?

Remember, reflections without action won't lead to transformation.

Let's get started!

The Blessed Journey

Let Him lead thee blindfold onwards,

Love needs not to know;

Children whom the Father leadeth

Ask not where they go.

Though the path be all unknown,

Over moors and mountains lone.

Give no ear to reason's questions;

Let the blind man hold

That the sun is but a fable

Men believed of old.

At the breast the babe will grow;

Whence the milk he need not know.

—GERHARD TERSTEEGEN, 1697–1769 (TR. UNKNOWN)

a known God

The desire to see what lies ahead lives within each of us. We wonder. We dream. We anticipate and hope. But at times we also worry. We fret. We fear. All that leads us to want to control events. When we lose our grip on control (which happens quite often since we aren't really in charge of things), anxiety appears. At times, it clutches us, taking our very breath.

This week, we will encounter the One who gives us our very breath. The One who spoke and created all we see and all we don't. The One who holds the universe together while we're worrying. The One who sees our future and is not shaken or surprised by any of it.

My prayer for us this week:

Almighty God,
Show us more of who You really are, not who we've made You to be. Open our eyes to see Your grandiosity. Your majesty. Your unique power and the ways You sustain the world. Exchange the graven images we've carved for You, the actual God who cannot be contained.
Amen.

INTRODUCTION TO WEEK 1
A KNOWN GOD

Remember the DeLorean? The plutonium-fueled, time-hopping machine that carried Marty McFly back in time? Let's be honest here. Wouldn't you love to have a shot at a little time travel? Maybe you'd like to go back in time and undo that thing you regret. Maybe then your current reality and future would look a little different. Or maybe what you really want is to jump a few years ahead and see how this thing you're waiting for pans out. You long to see how your kids grow up or if you get this job or if that relationship works.

Which direction would you go? Back or forward? The reality is we don't get to do either. It's just not possible. So we must live right here, right where we are in this current space and time.

In the absence of the ability to time travel, our view is limited. We can't go back and change past mistakes and we can't foretell the future. So we tend to try to control absolutely everything in the current moment to ensure that what happens next will be what we want: a future void of pain and a life free of suffering.

That kind of life existed in the very beginning in the beautiful land of Eden and it will exist again in the New Jerusalem, but for now, we're stuck—in the midst of the broken paradise.

Jesus told us we would indeed have trouble in this world. But He also said to take heart, for He has overcome the world—the broken paradise (John 16:33).

I know I can't control the future. I can't predict it. I can't force it to go a certain way, but I still try. Day after day I try to control what will happen. Then when I hit a wall where I can't, I end up in the downward spiral. Let me explain what I mean.

Person A (could be anyone—a spouse, a friend, a coworker, a family member) was supposed to call, but didn't.

We have two paths from this moment.

One path ends with "Something awful happened to Person A!"

The other path ends with "Person A hates me."

Sounds ridiculous, doesn't it? But it's what we do.

There's a gap between what we know and what we don't know. We are going to call that gap the unknown.

UNKNOWN

We try to fill in the unknown. How we do that is likely not entirely accurate, but we don't like having gaps in what we know, so we fill it in however we can. But we don't just jump all the way to the end; no, there are multiple stops along the way to get to these outlandish destinations.

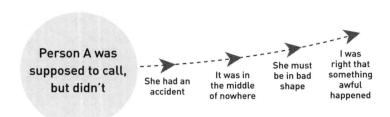

On the right side of the diagram are the external circumstances. Person A was supposed to call, but didn't, so now I imagine she had an accident. It was in the middle of nowhere, where there are no first responders. A is obviously in bad shape. So I was right that some terrible thing befell Person A. Sounds reasonable, right?

On the left side of the diagram are the internal circumstances. Person A was supposed to call, but didn't. Clearly, I've offended her by some comment I shouldn't have made. I'm such an idiot and just can't keep my mouth shut. She must be angry with me. Person A hates me.

These scenarios are certainly possible. They could happen. But the likelihood of it happening every single time the expected call doesn't come is slim. Yet if that is the case, why is it that our brains re-create this scenario so often?

In this downward spiral, we begin filling in the gap of the unknown, and once we begin traveling down this road, it spirals down and down. We can't stop it. At least it feels as though we can't. But we *can* learn to think differently.

When we dwell in the downward spiral, allowing it to shape how we view our reality, we've left out God, thinking He's nowhere to be found. We end up dwelling on the things we don't know and can't know. We've chosen to focus on the unknown, which breeds fear, instead of on what we *do* know. Just like the whispers of the Holy Spirit during my journaling, God asks us, "Tell Me what you *do* know."

What do we really need to know then? Do we need to know what our future looks like or do we need to know the One who holds it? Perhaps instead of trying to fill in the downward spiral gaps or hopping into a DeLorean, we need to walk hand in hand, step by step with the One who does know.

You see, God already knows our future. He's not bound by time.[3]

He's already ordained all our days before they have even come to be (Ps. 139:16). He's never surprised by your situation or mine. He's not pacing back and forth worried about what we've gotten ourselves into. No matter the circumstances, He sits on the throne, unchanged by our choices, without fear, and with a plan to redeem and restore us. *He knew me in the womb — Yet un-formed.*

When we align ourselves with God, understanding and knowing who He is, we experience a peace we will not find in trying to control our situation. God will not change (Ps. 55:19; James 1:17). *Every Good gift comes from God*

Maybe you've got the control thing down and it's working for you. You're rockin' your schedule and are determining outcomes right and left. At some point, however, it will break down. *It's also exhausting*, because we weren't meant to run the world. We weren't made to hold it all together. That's God's job, not ours. Sometimes I can't even run my own household, let alone the world!

When we think through the long list of unknowns, it's hard to understand why we would choose to dwell in the unknown when we worship a God who has made Himself known.

Remember that gap—the unknown? This week we will dive into Acts 17, where Paul encounters an altar built to an unknown god and boldly proclaims to the men of Athens the God who is known.

The people of Athens filled their city with idols, and Paul grieved at the sight of them. He first went to the synagogue to reason with the Jews there about the

3. Peter Kreeft, and Ronald K. Tacelli, *Handbook of Christian Apologetics: Hundreds of Answers to Crucial Questions* (Downers Grove, IL: InterVarsity Press, 1994), 93.

Messiah and at the town market with the God-fearing Greeks. But one day he had a different audience. Some Epicurean and Stoic philosophers overheard his vibrant discourse and entered the conversation. Calling him a babbler, they brought him before the Areopagus, a religious and educational council[4] in Athens, to explain the new teaching he shared. These philosophers spent a great deal of time eloquently trying to explain unknown things.

Paul described the Athenian desire to worship as seen in their religious attempts throughout the city. He explained how he had even found an altar with the inscription "TO AN UNKNOWN GOD" (Acts 17:23). This altar was used as a failsafe, just in case they missed one of the gods along the way.

But Paul did something remarkable that day. He took something unknown and showed how it had already been made known. He declared, "So you are ignorant of the very thing you worship—and this is what I am going to proclaim to you." Then Paul began to describe the living God:

> "The God who made the world and everything in it is the Lord of heaven and earth and does not live in temples built by human hands. And he is not served by human hands, as if he needed anything. Rather, he himself gives everyone life and breath and everything else. From one man he made all the nations, that they should inhabit the whole earth; and he marked out their appointed times in history and the boundaries of their lands. God did this so that they would seek him and perhaps reach out for him and find him, though he is not far from any one of us. 'For in him we live and move and have our being.' As some of your own poets have said, 'We are his offspring.'" (Acts 17:24–28)

Paul meets the men of Athens right where they are. He even proves himself as an amazing communicator in this moment when he references their own poets, speaking a language they understand immediately. He tells them about the grandeur of God, the way He cannot be contained. In a city where they created idols constantly, this truth is significant. If you make an idol, you must craft it with

4. Acts 17:19, *Areopagus* from the *Ryrie Study Bible* (Chicago: Moody, 2011), 1347.

your own two hands (Isa. 44:12), and who wants to worship something you can make yourself?

How often do we take the space of the unknown and fill it with something that isn't God? Something that has absolutely no power? We create and craft a false god or a false savior. God wasn't created—He *is* the Creator. He isn't fashioned—He alone fashions. When we worship Him, He doesn't say, "Thanks for the reminder, guys. I forgot that I was God." He has the ability to speak and create complex things. He doesn't need us, but because of His great love for us, He wants us and made a way for us to come into His presence and to have a personal relationship with Him.

Even in Paul's discourse, he reminds us that God's purpose in all this was so that we would seek Him and perhaps reach out for Him and find Him (Acts 17:27). He is both transcendent and immanent. He is majestic, powerful, above all, and simultaneously personal, near, and with us. It's astonishing to know and accept that a God who is *that* big and *that* powerful would want to have a relationship with someone like me. The reality is that God's message to us is, "I want you to know me. Since I cannot be in the presence of sin, I will cover you with the righteousness of My Son, Jesus. Then you can know Me."

The Greek language contains two definitions for the word *knowledge*. The first word is *gnosis*. This type is factual knowledge. These are things you know *about*. The second word is *epignosis*. This type is experiential knowledge. These are things we really truly know. It's the difference between knowing about a celebrity or acquaintance and knowing your spouse or children. In the experiential relationship, you anticipate needs. You understand glances. You have been a student of the person long enough to know and predict what they're thinking and feeling. You can't get to *epignosis* unless you go through *gnosis*. In our contemporary language, we sometimes differentiate these by calling them "head knowledge" (*gnosis*) and "heart knowledge" (*epignosis*).

The list I wrote in my journal were things I've experienced with God over time. I read about them first in His Word or heard stories from the experiences of others, but through the course of my journey with Jesus, I witnessed them for myself. He taught me those things in the peaks and valleys of my own walk with Him. Some of it I learned in the pit with Jesus. I had to stay there and allow Him to love me. I had to grab His hand and allow Him to do the work. We work it out in real life and in real time. It doesn't happen quickly.

As we grow in our *gnosis*—our factual knowledge of God—it should lead us to this *epignosis*—true experiential knowledge of God. That's the way God longs for us to know Him. God wants us to seek Him and find Him. The God of the universe— the One who cannot be contained—wants you to *know* Him. And He's made a way for that to happen.

LISTEN AND LINGER

Read through Acts 17:24–28. Write out the phrases that are the most meaningful to you.

What do you notice about God in this passage that speaks to your fear of the unknown?

He made me, knows me - Is in control of All the universe & wants me to seek him - to really know him & listen to Him

Remember how the Holy Spirit whispered to list what I did know instead of dwelling on what I didn't? If you made a list today, what would you put on it? Write what you do know. Place that list where you will see it often.

I Know God is Real
  "   "   He sent Jesus to Redieme
Us.
  I Know Christ died for me.
  " "   I accept Jesus as my
Saviour
  I Know God Loves me
  " "   He will always despite my
Sins.
I Know God ans. prayers
  " "   God will take care of me.
  " "   Know I will be saved from
eternal life & will see eternial Life

WEEK 1 | DAY 1

THE NAMING OF A KNOWN GOD

I imagine it was quite a scene. Paul, the preacher, philosophizing with the most educated in Athens. What a sight it must have been! The open air swarming with questions. The rhetoric dancing all around them. The quizzical glances peering from those accusing Paul of being a babbler even though deep in their souls they wondered about this God he was describing.

Today, we're going to spend some time sitting in this scene, asking God to stir our imaginations. What would it have been like to be right there with Paul? How would it have felt to be listening to the debate? What would the surroundings have been like? How would we have responded to Paul? To the questions of the Epicurean and Stoic philosophers?

The Athenian culture was very similar to ours, so it wouldn't be too hard to imagine what everyone was thinking or how Paul's explanation of who the "unknown god" is would have received starkly different reactions.

We're going to read this passage a couple of times, looking for the answers to the questions below during each reading.

Take some time to visualize what the scene was like. Read these words Paul spoke as if you were in the Areopagus searching for truth and it was the first you'd heard about the God he's describing. How would you respond?

Read through Acts 17:16–34 slowly with these questions in mind. After reading, set aside the text for a moment.

Now begin to imagine the scene as if you were right in the middle of it. Answer the following questions:

What do you see?

What do you hear?

What do you smell?

What's your position?

Who else is there with you?

What are you feeling?

What's the mood of the crowd?

What is your response to all of this?

What questions do you have?

What fears do you have?

Don't worry about historical accuracy. Just allow God to bring the story to life. These people we read about in Scripture were real people who walked the earth and had feelings and thoughts much like ours.

Write down some of the things you are noticing from your responses.

Now read through Acts 17:16–34 again.

Ask God to reveal to you what He wants you to see.

What are your observations about the text?

What is God calling you to do as a result of reading this passage?

Lord, You are the God who made the world and everything in it. You are the Lord of heaven and earth. I know You do not need anything, including me. I'm grateful You have chosen to have a relationship with me anyway. You are a God who has made Yourself known. Thank You for that truth. Help me to believe it and live what I know is true. Amen.

My Prayer:

Journaling Prompt:

What unknown am I facing right now? What do I need to know about God right now in the midst of the unknown? How have I seen God show Himself to me lately?

WEEK 1 | DAY 2

WHEN WE MAKE LITTLE GODS INSTEAD

The potter made it look so easy. The clay just obeyed his hands. What began as a mangled lump of slimy mud had become an exquisite vase that you could easily picture displaying vibrant flowers.

I looked at my own clump of wet dirt on the wheel and took a deep breath. The clay didn't quite obey when it was in my hands, and my novice ability produced the oddest-shaped mug you've ever seen. I suppose you could say it was quaint. It didn't quite look like the instructor's piece, but I was proud to have produced something with my own hands.

I'm no creator, that's for sure. I'm a manipulator of created things. The things I "create" don't really hold much power at all. But even though the instructor's finished product was more beautiful than mine, it didn't hold any power either. It had no control over itself or anything else. It could hold some water and flowers and that's about it.

Whenever I read about Israel's history of idol making, I typically have the same response: "What were you thinking?" The notion of the Israelites giving their gold jewelry for Aaron to shape into the golden calf seems ludicrous. What kind of power could a man-made calf hold? But they bowed down to it anyway (Ex. 32:1–35).

Forming idols seems like a crazy thing to do. Most of us aren't pouring our melted golden earrings into a calf mold and worshiping it. We're not blatantly crafting idols and then gathering groups of people to bow down to them.

But here's what we need to understand about idolatry: Idolatry includes any ultimate confidence in something other than God Himself.[5] When we put our

---

5. Allen C. Myers, *The Eerdmans Bible Dictionary* (Grand Rapids, MI: Eerdmans, 1987), 512.

confidence in anything other than Jesus, we have chosen idolatry. In other words, you and I craft idols anytime we place our trust in something other than God.

When we choose a comforter other than Jesus, we choose idolatry. When we take control of the situation instead of waiting on God, we choose idolatry. Isaiah shows us what it looks like when we choose this path.

Read through Isaiah 44:6–23 slowly in your own Bible. Mark any words or phrases that stand out to you. You can mark them in your Bible or write them down in a journal or in the space below. Notice the imagery Isaiah uses in this passage.

Read through the passage again. Contrast the characteristics of God with the characteristics of created idols and write them below.

CHARACTERISTICS OF

GOD

IDOLS

_____   _____
_____   _____
_____   _____
_____   _____
_____   _____
_____   _____
_____   _____

What do you notice about the characteristics you found?

List below some things you sometimes choose to place your trust in other than God. Ask the Holy Spirit to reveal these things to you.

Spend a moment confessing to God these idols, asking Him to take the place of your ultimate confidence.

Reread Isaiah 44:21–23.

Remember, when we turn our eyes back to Him, our Redeemer, He welcomes us with open arms. He is the Lord and there is no other (Isa. 43:1–11; 44:6; 45:5–6; Joel 2:27). That doesn't change even when we place other things on the throne. God is still God. His mercy and compassion for us do not fail even when we do. That's a God who's worth bowing down to.

Almighty God, help me to identify where I have created idols. Reveal to me the things I have placed before You. Forgive me for the ways I have not trusted in You for all things. You alone are God. You are my Rock and my Redeemer. Thank You for that truth. Help me to believe it and live what I know is true. Amen.

My Prayer:

Journaling Prompt:

What are your greatest idols? What would it take for you to lay them down? Take a moment to compare and contrast one of your "idols" with the living God. Make a chart of their differing characteristics. What do you notice? What invitation does God give to you as a result of reading the text for today?

WEEK 1 | DAY 3
POWERFUL KNOWLEDGE

Our daughter, Abigail, hates surprises. I'm talking *loathes* them, because she doesn't like not being in the know. We all like to be in the know.

It's said that knowledge is power. I think it depends on the kind of knowledge. My husband, Matt, is the kind of person who knows completely random facts about a lot of things. Some of these things are useful to know, but he also knows trivia that doesn't seem to have any point whatsoever. We'll be in a restaurant and he'll hear a song on the radio and quiz me with, "What band sang this song?" I usually have no clue. He knows every time. In my view, those seemingly useless tidbits of information contain little power unless you're a contestant on *Jeopardy!* and there is a category on bands.

The kind of knowledge that brings power is rooted deeply in our experience of something. We discussed the two different Greek words for knowledge:

Gnosis: the content of what is known—knowledge, what is known.[6]

This *gnosis* knowledge consists of the content—the facts, cognitive knowledge or "head knowledge" as some call it. Think about it as the facts without feelings. These are the things we know "about."

We can know God in this way—in a factual, statistical, cognitive way. Knowing facts about God is important, but data doesn't necessarily grow our faith in God when we are facing difficult circumstances. This sort of knowledge is where we begin when we are starting our journey with Jesus. We are to grow our cognitive knowledge because it leads us to an experiential knowledge.

Epignosis: the content of what is definitely known—what is known, definite knowledge, full knowledge.[7]

---

6. Johannes P. Louw and Eugene Albert Nida, *Greek-English Lexicon of the New Testament: Based on Semantic Domains* (New York: United Bible Societies, 1996), 335.
7. Louw and Nida, 335–36.

Epignosis refers to a more intimate knowledge—an experiential knowledge. This flavor of knowledge is not void of facts, but contains a more detailed understanding of the inner workings of the facts. There is a richer, more-rounded depth of familiarity.

Today we're going to read through four passages of Scripture with these two types of knowledge in mind. Our goal should be an *epignosis* knowing when it comes to God. This knowledge gives power to the believer—power over sin (Rom. 6) and power to become children of God (John 1:12). All power belongs to Christ (Matt. 28:18), but He has given it to those who follow Him (Luke 10:19), to those who truly "know" Him (John 10:14–15). This is the only kind of knowledge that can give true power.

Take a look at each of the four Scriptures below, noticing the different uses of the word "knowledge" as marked in each. Then answer the questions after each passage. (Note: *epignosis* is used in all words for "knowledge" in these passages except for the marked ones in 2 Peter 1:5).

His divine power has given us everything we need for a godly life through our **knowledge** of him who called us by his own glory and goodness. Through these he has given us his very great and precious promises, so that through them you may participate in the divine nature, having escaped the corruption in the world caused by evil desires.

For this very reason, make every effort to add to your faith goodness; and to goodness, **knowledge [gnosis]**; and to **knowledge [gnosis]**, self-control; and to self-control, perseverance; and to perseverance, godliness; and to godliness, mutual affection; and to mutual affection, love. For if you possess these qualities in increasing measure, they will keep you from being ineffective and unproductive in your **knowledge** of our Lord Jesus Christ. But whoever does not have them is nearsighted and blind, forgetting that they have been cleansed from their past sins.

Therefore, my brothers and sisters, make every effort to confirm your calling and election. For if you do these things, you will never stumble, and you will receive a rich welcome into the eternal kingdom of our Lord and Savior Jesus Christ. (2 Peter 1:3–11)

What stands out in the passage? Mark words or phrases.

What do you notice as you understand the nuances of the definition of the word "knowledge"?

What does this passage tell you about the knowledge you should grow?

How would that knowledge bring you power and ultimately peace according to these verses?

I keep asking that the God of our Lord Jesus Christ, the glorious Father, may give you the Spirit of wisdom and revelation, so that you may **know** him better. I pray that the eyes of your heart may be enlightened in order that you may **know** the hope to which he has called you, the riches of his glorious inheritance in his holy people, and his incomparably great power for us who believe. That power is the same as the mighty strength he exerted when he raised Christ from the dead and seated him at his right hand in the heavenly realms, far above all rule and authority, power and dominion, and every name that is invoked, not only in the present age but also in the one to come. And God placed all things under his feet and appointed him to be head over everything for the church, which is his body, the fullness of him who fills everything in every way. (Eph. 1:17–23)

What stands out in the passage? Mark words or phrases.

What do you notice as you understand the nuances of the definition of the word "knowledge"?

What does this passage tell you about the knowledge you should grow?

How would that knowledge bring you power and ultimately peace according to these verses?

> So Christ himself gave the apostles, the prophets, the evangelists, the pastors and teachers, to equip his people for works of service, so that the body of Christ may be built up until we all reach unity in the faith and in the **knowledge** of the Son of God and become mature, attaining to the whole measure of the fullness of Christ.
>
> Then we will no longer be infants, tossed back and forth by the waves, and blown here and there by every wind of teaching and by the cunning and craftiness of people in their deceitful scheming. Instead, speaking the truth in love, we will grow to become in every respect the mature body of him who is the head, that is, Christ. From him the whole body, joined and held together by every supporting ligament, grows and builds itself up in love, as each part does its work. (Eph. 4:11–16)

What stands out in the passage? Mark words or phrases.

What do you notice as you understand the nuances of the definition of the word "knowledge"?

What does this passage tell you about the knowledge you should grow?

How would that knowledge bring you power and ultimately peace according to these verses?

> For this reason, since the day we heard about you, we have not stopped praying for you. We continually ask God to fill you with the **knowledge** of his will through all the wisdom and understanding that the Spirit gives, so that you may live a life worthy of the Lord and please him in every way: bearing fruit in every good work, growing in the **knowledge** of God, being strengthened with all power according to his glorious might so that you may have great endurance and patience, and giving joyful thanks to the Father, who has qualified you to share in the inheritance of his holy people in the kingdom of light. For he has rescued us from the dominion of darkness and brought us into the kingdom of the Son he loves, in whom we have redemption, the forgiveness of sins. (Col. 1:9–14)

What stands out in the passage? Mark words or phrases.

What do you notice as you understand the nuances of the definition of the word "knowledge"?

What does this passage tell you about the knowledge you should grow?

How would that knowledge bring you power and ultimately peace according to these verses?

Heavenly Father, thank You for allowing me to truly know You. Thank You that I can experience Your presence and come to a greater understanding of who You are. Thank You that You are not far off, but are close and very near to me. Thank You for that truth. Help me to believe it and live what I know is true. Amen.

My Prayer:

Journaling Prompt:

How does it impact you that you can truly know the Lord? How have you experienced this knowledge in your own life? How would you like to grow your "true" knowledge of Christ? What would it take for you to do that?

WEEK 1 | DAY 4

WHAT DID SHE KNOW THAT I DON'T?

I remember dreaming about it when I was little. It began when I had the distinct privilege of being a flower girl in a beloved family friend's wedding. My dress twirled and sported the hottest color combination of the early eighties—dusty rose and powder gray. I remember imagining what it would be like when I got to be the bride.

I'm sure the same was true for Mary. I'm sure she had dreamed about her future, just like every other girl. But things for her changed drastically.

There she was, envisioning her upcoming wedding day. Like every little girl and like most brides, she was thinking about everything the day would hold. Would she feel like a princess? Would marriage be all she imagined it would be? What would life with Joseph be like?

In the middle of this dreamy moment, an unlikely messenger appears, proclaiming an unbelievable message that changes the course of everything for her.

Read Luke 1:26–38.

In an instant, Mary's entire world as she knew it turned upside down. All she'd dreamed of crumbled around her. Or at least, that's what I would have felt if I'd received that news.

But Mary's response is so very different. She listens and only asks a single question of the messenger.

"How will this be, since I am a virgin?" (v. 34)

I would have queried a million questions of Gabriel. How will Joseph respond?

How will I explain this situation to my parents? What are my friends going to think? Would I even still have friends? What will the town talk be? Who will speak to me after they discover this? Will I live through the scandal? Who will ever marry me now?

But that's just me.

She asks her simple, singular question. Gabriel replies with the answer explaining to Mary that nothing is impossible with God, that nothing He says will ever fail (v. 37).

That is enough for her.

She responds, "I am the Lord's servant. May your word to me be fulfilled" (v. 38). She goes from having one question to full surrender. Full surrender is something I've not achieved in my entire lifetime. Ever. First, I'm typically not satisfied with only asking one question. Second, full surrender is extremely difficult. It takes a great deal of trust.

As I read Mary's story in Luke 1, I find myself wondering: What did Mary *know* about God that allowed her to surrender so quickly? So fully? Clearly, Mary knew God. She didn't just know about Him. She was deeply familiar with Him. She had experienced His glory and power. She understood His provision. She had seen Him work in her life. She knew He was more than trustworthy.

When she visits her relative Elizabeth to share with her the news, she speaks a hymn of praise to God. Her song of surrender is filled with indications of her knowledge (*epignosis*) of God.

Read Mary's song of surrender in Luke 1:46–55.

As you read through Mary's song, what do you think she knew about God? Go line by line through this Scripture and write your response.

And Mary said:

"My soul glorifies the Lord
    and my spirit rejoices in God my Savior,
for he has been mindful
    of the humble state of his servant.
From now on all generations will call me blessed,
    for the Mighty One has done great things for me—
    holy is his name.
His mercy extends to those who fear him,
    from generation to generation.
He has performed mighty deeds with his arm;
    he has scattered those who are proud in their inmost thoughts.
He has brought down rulers from their thrones
    but has lifted up the humble.
He has filled the hungry with good things
    but has sent the rich away empty.
He has helped his servant Israel,
    remembering to be merciful
to Abraham and his descendants forever,
    just as he promised our ancestors."
(Luke 1:46–55)

What would your questions have been if you had received the news Mary or Joseph received regarding Jesus' birth? Would you have surrendered so quickly? If so, why? If not, why not?

God, You are enough. I know You are trustworthy. You are good—even when it feels as though the world is crashing down. You have a plan and nothing is impossible with You. Thank You for that truth. Help me to believe it and live what I know is true. Amen.

My Prayer:

Today, write your own hymn of praise to God, similar to Mary's.

Journaling Prompt:

When have your circumstances felt similar to Mary's—potentially hopeless or scandalous? What did you learn about God through those circumstances?

SOVEREIGN, POWERFUL CREATOR

Milk and cookies. Soup and salad. Bread and butter. Chips and guacamole. Macaroni and cheese. Peanut butter and jelly. Peanut butter and chocolate. Peanut butter and anything for me. (Sorry to those of you who have allergies. I just love my peanut butter!) These are great pairings.

Some other things are typically found together, but are not a great combination. Like anxiety and fear. These two are like a bad codependent relationship. Anxiety breeds fear and fear fuels anxiety. It's as though they just can't live without each other.

I don't know about you, but I'd like a lot less anxiety in my life. I'm finding these days that's just not something I can wish to happen. I can't simply breathe more deeply and expect anxiety to dissipate. It won't go away on its own.

Like Mary had, I long to forge a relationship with the Creator that will anchor me in tumultuous times. When the waves crash about, I want to still be standing. That's impossible to do on my own. But remember what Gabriel told Mary? Nothing is impossible with God (Luke 1:37 NASB). So, this isn't impossible either. *With Him it is possible.*

How do we even begin to think like the faithful men and women of the Bible whose trust ran deep? We start by spending time filling our own minds with truth. Truth about who God is and how He works. Truth about what He's done in the past. Truth about what His character is like. Truth about how He is good and has plans for us (Jer. 29:11).

We get to know Him through the printed pages of His Word.

Today we are going to engage in these truths in God's Word by using a four-part process where we will listen, linger, learn, and then see how we are to live as a result.

Today we will read through Psalm 104 four times. I know it might seem a little daunting at first, but I promise it will be worth it. God's Word always is. This way of studying Scripture is not about the repetition itself, but about digging deeper each time into the questions given. The intention is to peel back another layer of truth with each reading and each set of questions. God's Word can change us if we allow it. Let's begin!

LISTEN

Read through Psalm 104 in your own Bible. Sit quietly for a moment before you begin. Ask the Holy Spirit to speak and show you what the Lord wants for you in this passage. Mark words or phrases that stand out as you read in your Bible or write them in the space below or in your journal.

LINGER

Read the passage again out loud. Are the same words or phrases you marked the first time still standing out? Write them down. How do these words or phrases apply to your life right now?

LEARN

As you read the text for the third time, ask yourself these questions (you can write your answers here or in your journal):

How is God inviting me to respond? What does He want me to be learning from this? What am I noticing?

Read the passage one last time and answer these questions:

Why is God showing me this now?

What does this mean for my life?

How do I need to live differently?

How do I need to respond to God's invitation?

Lord God, You are the sovereign, powerful Creator. Your greatness and majesty are beyond my comprehension. I cannot begin to understand the vastness of Your reach. I believe You are in control of all that I can see and all that I can't. Thank You for that truth. Help me to believe it and live what I know is true. Amen.

My Prayer:

Journaling Prompt:

What did I learn about God today that I didn't know before? What was I reminded of that I had more than likely forgotten? What invitation is God extending to me today?

WEEK ONE: REFLECT AND ACT

We live in a fast-paced society where information flies at us nonstop. Typically, if our search results take more than a few seconds to load, we are off to the next site looking for the data we seek. Factual knowledge is readily available just about anywhere, even in a portal we carry in our pocket.

But what we're craving is experiential knowledge. We long for it in every relationship, including our relationship with God. That kind of knowledge needs time and space to sink into our core, to marinate within and change us.

Each week you'll have the opportunity to take a moment to reflect on what you've learned. Allow yourself some time to look back over your notes and journal entries, to see the answers you penned to the questions each day, and to revisit the new nuggets of truth the Scripture texts showed you. It will be worth it.

Take some time to answer each of these questions in your journal, or write your answers here:

What new truths did God reveal through my time in His Word this week?

What challenged me?

What am I still struggling to believe?

What are God's invitations to me right now?

Are there themes or patterns in what God is showing me? If so, what are they?

What action steps do I need to follow as a result of what I've learned this week?

Father, You giveth more grace when the burdens grow
  greater,
You sendeth more strength when the labors increase;
to added affliction You addeth Your mercy,
to multiplied trials Your multiplied peace.
When we have exhausted our store of endurance,
when our strength has failed ere the day is half done,
when we reach the end of our hoarded resources, Father
Your full giving is only begun.
Your love has no limit, Your grace has no measure;
Your power no boundary known unto men;
For out of Your infinite riches in Jesus, You giveth and
giveth and giveth again.[8]

"HE GIVETH MORE GRACE," ANNIE JOHNSON FLINT (1866–1932)

8. From Kurt Bjorklund, *Prayers for Today: A Yearlong Journey of Devotional Prayer* (Chicago: Moody, 2011), 79.

what do you really believe?

He replied, "You of little faith, why are you so afraid?" Then he got up and rebuked the winds and the waves, and it was completely calm. The men were amazed and asked, "What kind of man is this? Even the winds and the waves obey him!" MATTHEW 8:26–27

Knowing what we think we believe seems simple, but at times it's difficult to sift through our *actual* beliefs about God. This week we will discover a deeper meaning of the word "believe," helping to move us from thought to action. Belief affects the way we live. Some of our beliefs go unnoticed but affect our living in great ways.

I invite you to pray for God to reveal to you where your actual life isn't consistent with the beliefs you think you hold. Ask Him to show you what you *really* believe—especially where it is contradicting what the Word says is true about God's nature or character. God desires us to be people who believe deeply in who He is, allowing our knowledge of Him to shape our day-to-day living.

Remember, you will change at a rate that corresponds to the time you spend in the Word and at the feet of Jesus. The more intentional you are about spending time listening to Jesus through Scripture, pouring your heart out to Him through prayer, and noticing Him in your daily life, the more exponential your growth will be. Cultivating a daily discipline of meeting with Jesus takes time. And grace. And surrendered obedience. I'm praying you will see dividends quickly. Jesus is sufficient. For everything.

My prayer for us this week:

Lord Jesus,
We need You. We need You to reveal to us where our beliefs don't align with our actions. Open our eyes to see where we need to realign our beliefs and where we need to readjust our actions. Give us the grace we need to see what You see, the courage to step into change, and the power of the Holy Spirit to accomplish whatever You set before us. Amen.

INTRODUCTION TO WEEK 2

WHAT DO YOU *REALLY* BELIEVE?

It began like any other night on the water, I'm sure. The sun created a beautiful backdrop as it descended at the end of a long, hard day. The familiar water reflected the colors of the sky. A peaceful enough time for Jesus to lay down His weary head and surrender to sleep.

The boat rocked steadily with the waves. Back and forth. Back and forth. The fishermen dropped a net into the calm water to see what they might fetch for dinner. Nothing out of the ordinary. A perfect setting.

But as the men on the boat discovered soon enough, sometimes the perfect setting doesn't last very long. Raindrops. Wind. Then pouring, pounding rain and raging winds, whipping their equipment, tugging on them. Thunder, lightning. The boat no longer lapping serenely with the gentle waves, but now plummeting, then rising, over and over, out of control. Though this was a body of water the disciples knew well, and though they had logged hours and hours in their boats, and though this wasn't the first storm they'd seen while on the water . . . this one was different. This storm was just too big for them. They were frightened and needed a rescuer.

And what was Jesus doing through the raging rainstorm? He was *taking a nap*. The disciples' response sounds a lot like mine would have been: "Help us! Don't you care?" The disciples had specific expectations of how Jesus would respond. They thought since Jesus was with them, this shouldn't be happening. On top of it all, He was sleeping when He clearly should have been doing something about this frightening tempest!

They said the same thing I shout when I'm facing a wild tornado in my life. When something upsets the perfect scenario, I ask God if He even cares and what He's doing about the situation. The question comes in various forms. "Don't You hear me? Why is this happening? What are You doing about this?" When we ask these types of questions, we make an assumption that He doesn't care because we cannot see Him working on our terms. In the middle of the storm, what do we see? We see the storm. We see devastation. We fill in the unknown. But how many times have you reminded yourself in the midst of your own life storms to look back and see all the ways God was working for your good?

Our unknown is no different from the apostles' in that boat. No matter how big the storm or how small the boat, when Jesus is *with* us, we have nothing to fear. But that's difficult to remember at times, isn't it? When all you see is the wind and the waves, it's overwhelming.

The fishermen watched in awe as Jesus spoke in His recognizable voice, commanding the wind and the waves to hush. Their immediate response displayed His power over creation. They had witnessed Jesus preaching to the multitudes and healing the sick, but creation obeying His marching orders was something new for them. When I am afraid, Jesus could ask me the same questions He asked His disciples.

> Then Jesus turned to his wind-torn friends.
>
> "Why were you scared?" he asked. "Did you forget who I am? Did you believe your fears instead of me?"[9]

When we live in our fears, we have to wonder what we *really* believe about God. A. W. Tozer wrote, "What comes into our minds when we think about God is the most important thing about us."[10] What we believe about who God is affects how we respond.

The word "believe" is a tricky one. At times our understanding of *believe* doesn't venture past a mental thought. Our English definition means "to have confidence in the truth, the existence, or the reliability of something; to give credence to."[11] We tend to think about *what* we believe. It resides in our mind, not necessarily anywhere else.

---

9. Sally Lloyd-Jones, *The Jesus Storybook Bible* (Grand Rapids, MI: Zonderkidz, 2007), 242. Sally's rendering of this incident in Scripture is excellent for readers of all ages.
10. A. W. Tozer, *The Knowledge of the Holy* (New York: HarperOne, 1961), 1.
11. Believe. Dictionary.com. *Dictionary.com Unabridged*. Random House, Inc. http://www.dictionary.com/browse/believe.

The Hebrew and Greek understanding of *believe* contains another important dimension—it not only represents a mental assent, but comprises a three-part formula. The concept of *believe* in these languages includes a firm conviction producing an acknowledgment of God's revelation or truth, a personal surrender to that truth, and a conduct inspired by that surrender.[12] Belief begins in the mind, but doesn't stop there. Belief in the biblical sense is not simply a thought we have, but is a lived-out action.

When one believes something, he or she lives in recognition of that truth.

What we *actually* believe affects our everyday life. Our convictions shape our choices. They influence how we respond. When our actions are incongruent with what we regard as true, we must go back to the beginning and discover what we truly believe.

One of the core truths the disciples forgot in that boat during the downpour was that Jesus controlled creation. He *is* the Creator, holding things together (Col. 1:15–17). They believed their fear instead, and it changed their behavior. If they did remember who God was, they clearly thought He wasn't enough for their current situation. What do *you really* believe about God? Do you believe He is enough?

When we believe something, we *live* as though it is true. It's not just a word or a thought. If our *actual* life isn't lived in a way that proclaims what we believe, then we really don't believe it at all.

What do you really believe about God?

Do you believe God loves you? You cannot earn the love of God. We are saved by grace through faith. Not by works because then the focus would be our accomplishment and not God's work (Eph. 2:1–10). While we were still sinners, Christ demonstrated His love for us by dying on the cross (Rom. 5:8). God does not love us because we are lovable; He loves us because it's His nature to love us. God *is* love (1 John 4:8). Because of that truth, He cannot do anything *but* love us.

---

12. Believe. Hebrew "'aman." Greek "pisteuo." Preceptaustin.com. http://www.preceptaustin.org/hebrew_definitions.

You may not always *feel* like God loves you, but your feelings don't really get a say in the matter. God's love for you is a fact. It's a fact you can't do anything about. If you truly believe God loves you, how does it change the way you think and act? Think of the downward spiral, for example. Even if Person A hates me, I am loved by God and that is enough.

Do you believe God is for you? Romans 8:31 declares, "If God is for us, who can be against us?" Christ gave up His life for you. How much more "for" you could someone be? He is on your side. What would change about the way you think and act if you believed God is for you?

Do you believe God will give you what you need when you need it? God has access to it all. He owns and stewards all we can see and all we cannot. All things were made by Him and for Him and in Him all things hold together (Col. 1:15–17). He is in charge. Of everything. If He's in charge and He loves us, why would He not give us everything we need when we need it? Sometimes we *think* we need something that is simply a desire that is not the best for us. God wants what's best and will provide accordingly.

Do you believe God is always good? So many Scripture texts state it: the Lord is good (Ps. 145:9; 100:5; Lam. 3:24–26; Rom. 8:28). It's very easy for us to look around our current culture and think God is not good. How can there be suffering and pain in the world if God is good? This objection to God's goodness is put forward often.

We must remember something when we pose that question—we live in a broken Eden. Once sin entered the picture, this world is not the perfect place God created in the beginning. Yet God allows certain things to happen so we will seek Him and find Him (Acts 17:26–27). He's also constantly working toward redeeming and restoring everything, using it all for our good (Rom. 8:28), so He allows nothing that He doesn't already have a plan to redeem. (More about this during Week 5.)

I don't say that in a flippant way. This life is hard. It is hard when you have a frightening diagnosis. It is hard when your child has troubles. It is hard when your marriage fails. It is hard when a friendship dies. It is hard when you have a dream that doesn't come to fruition. Those things are hard for us and they break the heart of God. We live in a broken Eden, but God is still *always* good.

Do you believe God will never leave you? Believing this truth is complicated. Most of us have experienced rejection or someone walking away, and since we've been left by others, we don't trust God to stay. But that's not His character. Just like it's His character to love us, it's His character to never leave us (Heb. 13:5). There is nowhere we can go from His presence (Ps. 139:7–10). God won't abandon us. Ever. He is Emmanuel—God *with* us.

Do you believe God is in control of it all, holding it all together? Colossians 1:15–17 directly tells us Jesus holds all things together. Not some things or part of things, but *all* things. Jesus speaks and the winds and the waves obey. He made them, after all.

When we begin to believe all these truths, and we remember who God is, we forget our fears. Just like the waves in the storm, our anxiety begins to die down a little. When Jesus is *with* us, no matter how small the boat or how big the storm, we have nothing to fear. When we have nothing to fear, we can believe Jesus instead.

LISTEN AND LINGER

Read through Matthew 8:23–27.

What storms have you faced in your life in which you've felt as though Jesus were sleeping?

1 My Parents Divorce
2 Loss of my Mother father, step mom
3 This Election 2000

How did you see Him move through the storm?

1. Showing me I still had my Father in my Life
2. He reminded me I would see them again!
3. Reminder God is Control,... Period

What storms are you facing right now?

Still Election - I was reading in Acts and hearing a Bible study on Phone -
Rejoice in _all_ _Things_
Fear of what we Christians may Face Yet...

What are your questions for Jesus in the midst of them?

Why is Evil prevailing
Are we in the birth pains of the Last Days? Am I READY?

WEEK 2 | DAY 1

YOU ARE BIGGER

Springlike weather, the shining sun, and crisp air set the stage. It was a perfect day. We had an entire afternoon in Capernaum in Galilee. A chunk of time to sit with our feet in the same water Jesus sailed while we read Bible passages about events that took place in that very spot. We were in the area working with amazing church leaders who are doing ministry on the same soil where Jesus roamed.

While we soaked in the scenery along with the sunshine, we noticed the clouds shifting. They rose over the mountain range surrounding the water, darkening the once brightly lit sky. The backdrop changed dramatically. The black clouds gave way and the rain rolled through, pounding the rocks on the shore.

I would imagine it was mild compared to the day Jesus calmed the storm.

Today we're going to take a look at the main text for this week in two different accounts in the Gospels. We're going to read these passages a couple of times, looking for answers to the questions below with each reading.

Imagine the scene as if you were right in the middle of it. Read the story as if you were in the boat with the disciples.

Read Mark 4:35–41 and Matthew 8:23–27 in your own Bible and set it aside for a moment and consider the questions below:

What do you see?   *Rain - waves crashing - boat filling with water - The fear on others faces*

What do you hear?

Roar of the wind - Crys for safty - ~~holding on to side~~.

What do you smell?   *Salt*

What's your position in the boat?
Stern - close by it - Not in the rear

Who else is there?
Jesus, my friends

What are you feeling?
Scarred

What's the mood of the group?
Frightened

What do you think of all of this?
Death by drownding is here

What questions do you have?
Why Lord Now?

What fears do you have?
I'm not really ready to die,

Don't worry about historical accuracy. Just allow God to bring the story to life. The people we read about in Scripture were real people who walked the earth and had feelings and thoughts much like ours.

What are you noticing most? Write down your thoughts.

Only Christ is calm - All is hectic

What are your observations about the text?

Why were even his close so afraid

Remember the poignant questions Jesus asks in Sally Lloyd-Jones's version of this account in *The Jesus Storybook Bible*?

"Why were you scared?" he asked. "Did you forget who I Am? Did you believe your fears, instead of me?"[13]

How would you respond to this question? What fears are you believing instead of Jesus?

Yes I am - my Salvation

What do you need to remember about who God is in order to let go of those fears?

Believe in the Lord Jesus Christ & you will be Saved, Repent - Follow him trust his word.

13. Lloyd-Jones, *The Jesus Storybook Bible*, 242.

Lord Jesus, You control the wind and the waves. They know Your voice because they heard it at creation. There is not a single storm You cannot calm. You are bigger than any fear I face. Thank you for that truth. Help me to believe it and live what I know is true. Amen.

My Prayer:

Dear Lord, H Help me remember Your in Control of EVERY Thing! Calm my fears today & always - Ground me in your truths, Don't let Satan lead me into believing You are not with me.

Journaling Prompt:

Where have you believed your fears over believing Jesus? What do you need to ask of Him? When have you thought Jesus didn't care because He was silent? What is God inviting you to right now as a result of this passage?

WEEK 2 | DAY 2

YOU LOVE ME

Watch the hopeful young girl, plucking flower petals as she chants, "He loves me. He loves me not." This picture was the unfortunate description of my understanding of God's love for me for many years. If I did the right things enough times, I would then be worthy of God's love and, of course, He would have no choice but to love me. Because I was good.

But when I chose other, lesser things, I didn't understand how a disappointed God could love me at all. I didn't love myself then, so how could God love me? I believed that God's character—His choice of actions—were somehow affected by my behavior. I couldn't have been more deceived.

You see, God *is* love (1 John 4:8). His character cannot be affected by us. He is, after all, unchanging (Heb. 13:8). Remember that *big* God we read about last week who cannot be contained in a temple built by human hands? Our choices don't change who God is. He's just bigger than that. He will always be love and there is nothing we can do to change that.

He loved me before I even chose Him. While I was still sinning and unworthy, Jesus gave His life for me (Rom. 5:8). Why? Because He was demonstrating His great love for me.

He did the same for you. He loves you when you choose His way and He loves you when you don't. His love is unaffected by our behavior. Sure, He longs for us to be in a right relationship with Him and to be conformed into His image, but God's love is immovable. Unshakable. Always.

Today we're going to use the SOAP study method of engaging with Scripture. Here's how it works:

S for Scripture: Read slowly through the Scripture.

O for Observations: What are your observations about the text? What do you notice? What stands out?

A for Application: How is God calling you to apply the truth in this Scripture to your life right now? What is He calling you to change? How is He inviting you to be different?

P for Prayer: What can you pray as a result of what God is calling you to do in this passage? What do you need to praise God for or request of Him in response?

Let's dig into today's text!

S for Scripture:
Read slowly through Psalm 103:1–14 in the New Living Translation.

> Let all that I am praise the LORD;
>> with my whole heart, I will praise his holy name.
> Let all that I am praise the LORD;
>> may I never forget the good things he does for me.
> He forgives all my sins
>> and heals all my diseases.
> He redeems me from death
>> and crowns me with love and tender mercies.
> He fills my life with good things.
>> My youth is renewed like the eagle's!
>
> The LORD gives righteousness
>> and justice to all who are treated unfairly.
>
> He revealed his character to Moses
>> and his deeds to the people of Israel.

The Lord is compassionate and merciful,
    slow to get angry and filled with unfailing love.
He will not constantly accuse us,
    nor remain angry forever.
He does not punish us for all our sins;
    he does not deal harshly with us, as we deserve.
For his unfailing love toward those who fear him
    is as great as the height of the heavens above the earth.
He has removed our sins as far from us
    as the east is from the west.
The Lord is like a father to his children,
    tender and compassionate to those who fear him.
For he knows how weak we are;
    he remembers we are only dust.

O for Observation:

What are your observations about the text? What do you notice? What stands out?

> Rejoice in the Lord.
> Praise Him - Daily - thru all.
> His Love for me is Never Ending
> I don't deserve it But He still
> Loves me

With your observations in mind, read the following passages in your own Bible:

Isaiah 43:1–5
Romans 5:6–8
Ephesians 2:4–6
Romans 8:38–39

What do you notice? What stands out?

Gods Love for me
I am a sinner but He still Loves me
Nothing can change that

A for Application:

How is God calling you to apply the truth in these Scriptures to your life right now? What is He calling you to change? How is He inviting you to be different?

Nothing can seperate Me from Gods Love - He is with me to the End here and for Eternity with him

P for Prayer:

Heavenly Father, I know Your Word says You love me. Sometimes it's difficult to fully believe that truth, but You DO love me. You loved me before I chose You, when I was still a sinner. There is nothing that will separate me from Your love for me. Ever. Thank You for that truth. Help me to believe it and live what I know is true. Amen.

My Prayer:

What can you pray as a result of what God is calling you to do in this passage? What do you need to praise God for, confess to God, or request of Him in response?

Lord Help me in my unbeliefe
forgive my doubts of your Love
If I confess my Sins you are rightous
Just + forgive my Sins.

Nothing - No Person - Laws - Govt.
even the very control of the Earth is
in Gods Hands.
Praise to God. I have Nothing
to fear -- He is with me & Loves me

Journaling Prompt:

Do you believe God truly loves you unconditionally? If so, what helps you stay grounded in that belief? If not, what keeps you from embracing that truth? How would your life change if you believed God loved you? How would believing this truth affect how you approach the "unknown" places in your life?

Yes I do -
What Keeps me grounded?
Reading His Holy Word
So I can remember His Promises
always

WEEK 2 | DAY 3

YOU WILL NEVER LEAVE ME

It was the end of an era. Israel's season of wandering was coming to a close. With the days of manna and dusty feet diminishing, the Promised Land was not a far-off dream anymore. Moses had been training Joshua for a while, but now with Moses gone, it was Joshua's turn.

I'm not sure what sorts of fears Joshua had, but mine would have been tremendous. I would have doubted my ability to lead. I would have been afraid of conquering the territory ahead. I would have wondered if what we had was enough. I would have been afraid of failure, especially following someone like Moses. I would have been desperate for God to carry us all.

I've heard it said that courage isn't a lack of fear, but courage means moving forward even in the face of fear. It's choosing to be brave when fear rises up. In the passage for today, God reminds Joshua he can be strong and courageous because He will never leave him. Ever.

The same is true for us. We can certainly leave God if we choose; after all, we've been given free will in our relationship with Jesus, but He will never abandon us. Ever.

Today we're going to use the Listen, Linger, Learn, and Live questions to engage our text.

LISTEN

Read through Joshua 1:1–11 in your own Bible. Sit quietly for a moment before you begin. Ask the Holy Spirit to speak and show you what the Lord wants for you in this passage. Mark words or phrases in your own Bible that stand out as you read.

LINGER

Read the passage again out loud. Are the same words or phrases you marked the first time still standing out? Write them down. How do these words or phrases apply to your life right now?

VS5 No man shall stand against thee - I will not fail thee or forsake thee
VS6 Be strong & of good courage
VS-7 Be strong & courages - keep my comandments - meditate on then
8 turn neither right nor left

LEARN

As you read the text for the third time, ask yourself, How is God inviting me to respond? What does He want me to be learning from this? What am I noticing? Write out what comes to mind.

Be strong - courages, BE NOT AFRAID
The Lord your God is WITH Thee
where ever I go

LIVE

Read the passage one last time and answer these questions:

Why is God showing me this now?

God keeps His promises, I need to believe this to recieve His blessings

What does this mean for my life?

Trust God - DO NOT FEAr, His Word is True - He will be with me no matter what Happen-
He will Love Me

How do I need to live differently?

Be bold, trust, Have no fear Study Gods Word daily

How do I need to respond to God's invitation?

Prayer - Study, Faith

PRAYER FOR THE DAY

Almighty God, You will not leave me. You will not abandon me. You will be with me wherever I go. No matter the fear I face, You will not let me go. Your presence is constantly accessible to me through the power of the Holy Spirit. Thank You for that truth. Help me to believe it and live what I know is true. Amen.

My Prayer: *Lord, Thank You! For your Love, your Patience, your words of Faith & Wisdom in the Bible. Thank You for Showing me now what I had forgotten Thank You for leading back to You*

Journaling Prompt:

How does knowing God will never leave you change how you view the unknown spaces in your life? How does it calm your fears? What would help you remember this truth and live as though it is true?

Yes

WEEK 2 | DAY 4

YOU ARE FOR ME AND ARE ALWAYS GOOD

In the battle to believe, I'm discovering a tricky little obstacle. *Feelings.*

Ugh.

Some people read that word and think, "What are those?" Others of us know all too well what they are. Sometimes my feelings overwhelm me. I'm an artist and I work with artists, so I see (and unfortunately at times experience) firsthand the full gamut of possible emotions we can experience. I have a love/hate relationship with them. At times, they drive my passion for the kingdom and allow me to express artistically the love of God with deeper conviction. At other times, feelings cripple me.

Here's what I'm learning: feelings are not facts. Lysa TerKeurst explains in *Unglued* that "feelings are indicators, not dictators."[14] In other words, feelings don't get to tell me what to do or what to believe. They don't always tell the whole truth. A feeling might tell me I'm tired or there's an issue I need to address or I have some work to do. But what it doesn't tell me is the entire truth.

You see, a lot of times I don't *feel* like God is for me. I don't always *feel* like God is always good. *But He is.* I can't trust my feelings or lack of feelings to shape the truth. I have to learn to trust what the Bible says is true.

I'm finding that feelings will often follow facts over time. When I begin dwelling on the truths found in Scripture, they take root in my heart and then begin to inform my feelings.

Maybe you, like me, have trouble believing these things. Maybe you have trouble

14. Lysa TerKeurst, *Unglued: Making Wise Choices in the Midst of Raw Emotions* (Grand Rapids, MI: Zondervan, 2012), 72.

believing God is *always* good and is *always* for you. My prayer is that you will encounter these Scriptures today and will begin to write them on your heart—even if you're not feeling like they're true and you're struggling to believe them. We have to start somewhere, right? And over time God will grow our experiential knowledge of Him (*epignosis*), and that knowledge will transform our feelings.

Let's take a look at a series of passages that tell us God is good. Read through these, circling the words that describe God. Mark where the texts declare God is good.

I say to myself, "The Lord is my portion;
therefore I will wait for him."

The Lord is good to those whose hope is in him,
to the one who seeks him;
it is good to wait quietly
for the salvation of the Lord. (Lam. 3:24–26)

The Lord is good and does what is right;
he shows the proper path to those who go astray. (Ps. 25:8 NLT)

Enter his gates with thanksgiving
and his courts with praise;
give thanks to him and praise his name.
For the Lord is good and his love endures forever;
his faithfulness continues through all generations. (Ps. 100:4–5)

Then I called on the name of the Lord:
"Please, Lord, save me!"
How kind the Lord is! How good he is!
So merciful, this God of ours!
The Lord protects those of childlike faith;
I was facing death, and he saved me. (Ps. 116:4–6 NLT)

> You are my God, and I will praise you;
>> you are my God, and I will exalt you.

> Give thanks to the Lord, for he is good;
>> his love endures forever. (Ps. 118:28–29)

> The Lord is merciful and compassionate,
>> slow to get angry and filled with unfailing love.
> The Lord is good to everyone.
>> He showers compassion on all his creation. (Ps. 145:8–9 NLT)

What do you notice in what you marked? Do you believe these things to be true about God?

yes

It's difficult at times to believe God is for us, but He is. Using the SOAP method of Scripture study, dig into these Scriptures and let's see what God reveals through His Word.

S for Scripture:

Read slowly through the following Scriptures in your own Bible.

Deuteronomy 20:1–4
Romans 8:28–31
Psalm 27:1–3

O for Observation:

What are your observations about the text? What do you notice? What stands out?

God is with me
Be bold
Do not be Afraid, no matter who or what comes againt me.
The Lord is my strength. Salvation
I have No reason to fear Any Thing because God is on my side!

A for Application:

How is God calling you to apply the truth in these Scriptures to your life right now? What is He calling you to change? How is He inviting you to be different?

Pray
Praise
Trust
Believe

I have to ~~Resone~~ Reason to be afraid - Ever

P for Prayer:

Heavenly Father, because You are for me, I have nothing to fear. You fight for me when I cannot fight for myself. You shelter me when trouble comes. Even when I don't feel it, You are always good. Thank You for that truth. Help me to believe it and live what I know is true. Amen.

My Prayer:

What can you pray as a result of what God is calling you to do in these passages? What do you need to praise God for, confess to God, or request of Him in response?

Dear Lord, Thank You for the gift of this Bible Study & group. I Know you were Speaking to Naomi to invite me. Thank You, I will never again forget your word (With your help) I will Remember always I have no reason to fear for you are in Total Control of my life. And the intire World. Thank You

Journaling Prompt:

Where have you seen God fight for you in your life? Do you believe God is for you? Where have you seen evidence of this truth in your life? How often do you believe your feelings over the facts? What is God inviting you to change today?

He Fought for me when my life Lay in the balance.
He answered my prayers For John's life.
He fulfilled His promise when I had fallen away from Him & he brought me back.
I need to stop looking at the World & Keep my eyes on Him.

YOU ARE ENOUGH FOR ME

Piles and piles of papers lined the house; bulging boxes of unused, neglected things were heaped in the living room. Only a single pathway, like a road to nowhere, allowed those living there to walk from room to room.

My heart just ached for them. How does something like this happen? The hosts worked with them to clean the clutter, helping them release the many things they were clenching. Whenever I watch an episode of *Hoarders*, I always have a little pang of guilt for my own attachment to my collection of stuff.

More. More. More. It seems like a constant battle in so many areas of life. Everywhere we turn in American culture, more is available. If you don't have access to it all, you must be missing out. Isn't it crazy what the fear of missing out can do to us?

Sometimes my fear of missing out leads me to stockpile all kinds of things I fear I won't have when I need them. Toilet paper, shampoo, gift bags on sale, greeting cards, office supplies. Random things. Because, you know, those are the things that will sustain you when it really matters.

But then I also try to store up things you can't possibly even save. It just doesn't make sense. Things like grace. And mercy. God's love and forgiveness. As if they will run out. It's all fueled by fear of scarcity.

Scarcity is defined as "insufficiency or shortness of supply."[15] In other words, things will run out. What we have will not be enough. For example, at our family gatherings when my mom makes mashed potatoes, there is a scarcity mindset. With my middle brother around, you'd better take a giant heap of potatoes on the first helping because there may not be any left when he's done.

---

15. Scarcity. Dictionary.com. *Dictionary.com Unabridged*. Random House, Inc. http://www.dictionary.com/browse/scarcity.

What do we do when we have this mindset? We hoard. We're selfish. We're greedy. We might even help ourselves to what's not ours to take. We live in fear about the resource being gone. We plan and control, making sure we will have enough.

Our dread of scarcity is rooted in fear. We fear that our needs will not be met. This outlook reveals a lot of what we believe about God. *In scarcity, we put ourselves in the seat of the Savior.* We control the outcome. We are the ones who will have to come up with a solution to fix things or meet needs. We don't rely on the resources of God. He's just not enough.

Here's the truth you and I need to cling to: *our God is enough for us.* His resources are limitless. Psalm 50:9–11 says, "I have no need of a bull from your stall or of goats from your pens, for every animal of the forest is mine, and the cattle on a thousand hills. I know every bird in the mountains, and the insects in the fields are mine." *Everything* in all of creation belongs to God. It is His. He is a God of abundance, not of scarcity. Remember, scarcity is defined as "insufficiency or shortness of supply." God is not short on any supplies. Ever.

As you read through the texts today using Listen, Linger, Learn, and Live, examine your own tendency toward scarcity. Do you believe God will supply all of your needs? Are you, like Paul in Philippians 4:11–12, content with what He is giving you? Do you believe He is enough for you?

LISTEN

Read Matthew 6:25–34. I've included verses 25–34 below from the New American Standard Bible (for the entire passage, go to biblegateway.com and select the NASB option).

Sit quietly for a moment before you begin. Ask the Holy Spirit to speak and show you what the Lord wants for you in this passage. Mark words or phrases that stand out as you read. (FYI: In the New American Standard Bible, this passage is titled, "The Cure for Anxiety." Funny, huh?)

For this reason I say to you, do not be worried about your life, as to what you will eat or what you will drink; nor for your body, as to what you will put on. Is not life more than food, and the body more than clothing? Look at the birds of the air, that they do not sow, nor reap nor gather into barns, and yet your heavenly Father feeds them. Are you not worth much more than they? And who of you by being worried can add a single hour to his life? And why are you worried about clothing? Observe how the lilies of the field grow; they do not toil nor do they spin, yet I say to you that not even Solomon in all his glory clothed himself like one of these. But if God so clothes the grass of the field, which is alive today and tomorrow is thrown into the furnace, will He not much more clothe you? You of little faith! Do not worry then, saying, "What will we eat?" or "What will we drink?" or "What will we wear for clothing?" For the Gentiles eagerly seek all these things; for your heavenly Father knows that you need all these things. But seek first His kingdom and His righteousness, and all these things will be added to you.

So do not worry about tomorrow; for tomorrow will care for itself. Each day has enough trouble of its own.

LINGER

Read the passage again out loud. Are the same words or phrases you marked the first time still standing out? Write them down. How do these words or phrases apply to your life right now?

Do Not be worried x Life, food, Clothing God will take care of our need

Do Not Worry, The world does that, they don't Know God,

Seek God first, His Kingdom x His righteousness - You will recieve all you need

Do Not worry about tomarrow! It will take care of itsself.

As you read the text for the third time, ask yourself, "How is God inviting me to respond? What does He want me to be learning from this? What am I noticing?" Write out what comes to mind.

God is in Control - He ownes every thing on Earth. He is good, He will supply my needs, My worry does no good + it stills my joy.

LIVE

Read the passage one last time and answer these questions:

Why is God showing me this now?

I'm very guilty of trying to take care of myself and forgetting this

What does this mean for my life?

Turn Loose + Have ~~Peace~~ Peace

How do I need to live differently?

Thru Faith + Prayers, trusting God to Supply ~~~~ all my needs

How do I need to respond to God's invitation?

Prayer + Bible Study to Keep my mind right -
Praise + Thankfullness to God
Start Cleaning out Closets ect.. Someone else
Could use my Stuf that needs it !

Heavenly Father, at times, I struggle to believe You will provide all I need. It's hard sometimes to believe what I cannot see. Grow my faith in You. Grow my trust in Your provision. You own it all. You have no needs. You are the Creator AND Sustainer. You are enough for me. Thank You for that truth. Help me to believe it and live what I know is true. Amen.

My Prayer: *Lord, Help me remember to put my Faith in You, not myself. To study & Learn From Your word Daily. Remembering always You Love me & will Supply all my Needs!*

Journaling Prompt:

Do you have a scarcity or an abundance mentality? How does this affect your relationship with God? What is God inviting you to believe today? Remember, gratitude is the gateway to believing God will provide. Take some time to begin a gratitude list in your journal. Write down at least ten things that stir gratitude in your heart. Add to the list often.

I will have abundance from Now on w/ Gods Help. Trusting in His word & Mercy.

1. My Salvation
2. My Home
3. " Family
4. " Friends
5. " My Animals
6. Health
7. Food
8. Clothing
9. Safty
10. My Boys
11 Grand sons

WEEK TWO: REFLECT AND ACT

We've digested a lot this week. Looking at what we actually believe reveals a lot, doesn't it? Remember, your relationship with Christ is a journey. Journeys are traveled one step at a time. Regardless of what you discovered about the deficiencies in your beliefs this week, grace is yours. Jesus is still crazy about you, delights in the fact you are His, and loves you deeply.

When we discover new opportunities for growth, taking the time to reflect and choose some next steps is vital. Maybe God revealed something remarkable to you this week. Don't let that go unnoticed! Take some time to allow it to settle in. Maybe this week overwhelmed you and you don't even know where to begin. Regardless of your experience this week, take a moment to answer the questions and choose just one action step.

Take some time to answer each of these questions in your journal or in the space below:

What new truths did God reveal through my time in His Word this week?

I need more Faith & Trust in God & his Word
I have NO Reason to worry & Fret

What challenged me?

To Let go of All my many fears!
Trust God 100%

What am I still struggling to believe?

That God still Loves me

What are God's invitations to me right now?

Pray & Thank Him for His love

Are there themes or patterns in what God is showing me? If so, what are they?

Do Not Worry God will supply All my needs

What action steps do I need to follow as a result of what I've learned this week?

When in doubt & fear slips into me - worry - Stop - Read the Word & trust

Remember that awakening to the Holy Spirit's invitations takes time. It takes stopping long enough to listen. It takes space to take a deep look at how we're operating. I'm praying you will begin to *really* believe the truths about our amazing God we've encountered this week and you will live as though they are true.

Amen

I arise today through God's strength to pilot me,

  God's might to uphold me,

  God's wisdom to guide me,

  God's eye to look before me,

  God's ear to hear me,

  God's word to speak for me,

  God's hand to guard me, . . .

  God's shield to protect me,

  God's hosts to save me

from snares of the devil, from temptations of vices,

from every one who desires me ill, . . .

Christ with me, Christ before me, Christ behind me,

Christ in me, Christ beneath me, Christ above me,

Christ on my right, Christ on my left,

Christ when I lie down, Christ when I sit down . . . [16]

—PATRICK, IRISH MISSIONARY (387–493)

16. From Kurt Bjorklund, *Prayers for Today: A Yearlong Journey of Devotional Prayer* (Chicago: Moody, 2011), 99.

cornerstone

You also, like living stones, are being built into a spiritual house to be a holy priesthood, offering spiritual sacrifices acceptable to God through Jesus Christ. For in Scripture it says: "See, I lay a stone in Zion, a chosen and precious cornerstone, and the one who trusts in him will never be put to shame." 1 PETER 2:5-6

Over the past two weeks, we've discussed how God has made Himself known and what it means to know Him at a deeper, more experiential level (*epignosis*). We've dug into our core belief systems and examined how those affect the choices we make every day.

Since we're talking about our belief system, it's time to examine the foundation on which it's all built—our cornerstone. What we build our life upon matters a great deal. It affects everything.

It's easy to think we've built our life on Jesus alone, but in reality, at times we've chosen lesser things in which we place our hope and trust, sometimes without even being fully aware of it. Everything besides Jesus will fall and fail when placed in the position rightly belonging to Him. He's the only One capable enough and powerful enough to hold that place.

My prayer for us this week:

Lord Jesus,
Help us to have the courage to look honestly at the foundation we've built for our lives. Give us eyes to see where we've laid down hollow cornerstones. We want our hope to be built on You, Jesus, nothing else. Reveal to us where we've placed our hope in other things. Give us Your grace and Your mercy as we dig up false foundations. Help us remember You alone are God.
Amen.

INTRODUCTION TO WEEK 3
CORNERSTONE

The words swirled in the air like dandelion seeds in the warm summer breeze, the melody lingering as we sang the lyrics with bold fervor. "My hope is built on nothing less than Jesus' blood and righteousness; I dare not trust the sweetest frame, but wholly lean on Jesus' name."[17] It sounds like such a great sentiment, doesn't it? Me, trusting in *nothing* other than the name of Jesus. If only that were completely true all the time.

I found myself wondering, "Is my hope really built on nothing other than Jesus? Am I trusting in His righteousness alone and not trying to earn my own? Am I leaning *fully* on His name and not myself?"

Most days, only a slim chance exists that I am hoping in Jesus and nothing else. I'm going to take a leap of faith and guess that it's probably the same for you. How do we move to where these rousing words take root and become the truth we're living?

First, we have to take a look at where our hope is rooted. What comes to mind when I ask, "Where do you put your hope?" The Sunday school–churchy answer is, of course, "Jesus," but we've already established there are most likely things other than Jesus in which we place our hope. So what would those things be? Here's a simple list I believe many of us can relate to:

- *Accomplishments*
- *Spouse*
- *Children and their success and/or failure*
- *Church*
- *Bank accounts*
- *Career*

17. "Solid Rock" by Edward Mote, http://hymnary.org/text/my_hope_is_built_on_nothing_less.

- *Relationships*

- *Abilities and talents*

- *Possessions*

- *Experiences (e.g., vacations, trips, ability to go and do things)*

I'm sure you're thinking, "Laura, those are all great things! How could it be wrong for me to put my hope in them?" They're not bad things in themselves. We want our marriages to be healthy. We want our children to be successful. We want deep relationships with others. We want to be a part of a church community that reminds us of who we are in Christ and guides us as we're transformed into His image. These are all wonderful things, of course, but when they are more a priority than Jesus Himself or exert influence greater than Jesus Himself, they become an idol—something we are looking to for something only Jesus can give. Let me explain.

Some of us place our hope in our spouse or significant others. We look to those relationships to provide security and identity and worth instead of for companionship and opportunities to grow into the likeness of Christ. We can trust our jobs and careers to help us pay the bills, but all too often, we make our careers the bedrock of our existence. So much so that, if we lose a job, we don't know how to define ourselves.

One of the hardest areas can be in the parenting department. Ugh, if parenting isn't a mirror for our souls, I'm not sure what is! If you're a parent, perhaps you've had to go to a meeting with your child's teacher, or even with the principal or the guidance counselor. Perhaps you've wondered what these professionals must think about you as a parent. It felt like *you* were the one getting a report card—for your parenting.

Maybe that doesn't bother you and you don't really care what people think about this or another area of life, but when your bank account gets below a certain level, you just can't handle it. Or perhaps you are so thrown by whoever is in political office that you can't breathe when you think about it. Maybe you think one more vacation or one more "toy" will calm your fears. Maybe you trust your abilities and talents to carry you through every situation, and that's where your hope lies.

Regardless of your preferred source of hope, if it's not Jesus, it will disappoint. Jobs are lost. Bank accounts drain. Spouses make mistakes. Human relationships fail. Children will inevitably make wrong choices. Politicians . . . well, I'm just going to leave that one completely alone. Vacations and toys are fun, but their novelty wears off. Our abilities and talents can't always be trusted. After all, what happens when we can no longer do the things we once did or if someone comes along who can do tasks a bit better than we can?

None of these things were meant to be our only hope. Our hopes become what our life is built upon. These things become our cornerstone.

Paul had something to say to the Ephesians about choosing a cornerstone. In Ephesians 1:18–23, Paul encourages the Ephesians to remember the hope to which they were called.

> I pray that the eyes of your heart may be enlightened in order that you may know the hope to which he has called you, the riches of his glorious inheritance in his holy people, and his incomparably great power for us who believe. That power is the same as the mighty strength he exerted when he raised Christ from the dead and seated him at his right hand in the heavenly realms, far above all rule and authority, power and dominion, and every name that is invoked, not only in the present age but also in the one to come. And God placed all things under his feet and appointed him to be head over everything for the church, which is his body, the fullness of him who fills everything in every way.

Paul speaks of the hope we've been given, the inheritance that belongs to us as God's holy people. We even have access to the same power that raised Christ from the dead. Paul reminds us also of Christ's position over all things in creation.

Through chapter 2, he reviews what we once were and now are. We once were sinners, now we are forgiven. We once were dead, we've now been made alive. We once belonged to the ruler of the kingdom of the air, but now we belong to God Himself.

All this is not of our own doing, but through the grace of Jesus Christ and His work on the cross. We are merely recipients of a gift we did not deserve.

As Paul continues, he declares we now have access to the Father because of Jesus. Then he goes on to solidify our identities as well as our futures in Ephesians 2:19–22:

> Consequently, you are no longer foreigners and strangers, but fellow citizens with God's people and also members of his household, built on the foundation of the apostles and prophets, with Christ Jesus himself as the chief cornerstone. In him the whole building is joined together and rises to become a holy temple in the Lord. And in him you too are being built together to become a dwelling in which God lives by his Spirit.

If we've been given a hope of a glorious inheritance in Christ, our cornerstone must be Christ Himself. We cannot hope in anything other than the person of Jesus. What we are becoming is directly related to what we're choosing as our foundation.

To understand what we're being built upon, we're looking at this key word, *cornerstone*, and what the concept entails. What is a cornerstone? Every building has one.

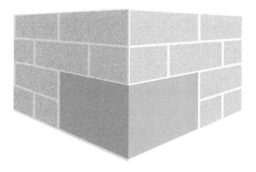

In architecture, the cornerstone is the first stone of a building that is set in place. It's the stone that determines the way the rest of the building will be built. Every other stone is completely dependent on the direction and setting of the corner-stone, since it is the block that sets the trajectory for every other stone. If it's not set just right, all the other stones will be out of balance.

Another concept of cornerstone is one that's been developed over time, but is only for show. If you look on the side of certain buildings, you will find a ceremonial masonry stone set in a prominent location on the outside of the building. Typically, there is an inscription on this stone denoting the construction dates and names of the builders. This type of stone is purely cosmetic and has absolutely no bearing on the building's construction at all.

Which kind of cornerstone are we allowing Jesus to be in our life? Is He the *first* stone set? Are we allowing Him to determine everything else in our lives? Do we allow Him to lead, or must we be in control? Are we dependent on Him? For example, on what basis do we make decisions? Some are easy: chicken or pasta? Pants or the skirt? But other decisions are foundational, made according to the cornerstone of our lives, which should be Jesus.

You are the dwelling place of Christ. He is building *you* into the building. You *are* being built into it whether you think about it or not. You have chosen a cornerstone whether you've thought about it or not. Your life doesn't function in isolation. *You're building a wall of the church with your life.* How does that work if you don't put Jesus into the cornerstone position?

When you choose Jesus as the stone that determines every other stone, your witness to the world changes. Your relationships change. Your hopes change too. That situation with your child at school? When Jesus is your cornerstone, you understand He is already working to redeem and restore all things. You remember He loves your child even more than you do. You trust what He says is true about your parenting and not how others may choose to see you.

Suddenly the way you think about everything else changes. Your perspective sees Jesus first.

Let's add another architectural term: the *keystone*. The keystone on an arch is the central stone at the top that holds the other stones in place. Think of it as key to holding the arch in place and what would happen if it were removed. If we're putting our hopes in anything besides Christ as our foundation, that is, our cornerstone—such as our career, relationships, bank balance, or anything else on that list a few pages back—our building will crumble. If we're looking for something other than Christ to be the stone that holds it all together, you won't find anything. When trouble comes, it's none of those things that will hold it all together. They can't.

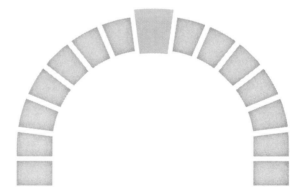

But Jesus can. We're told in Colossians 1:15–17 that in fact this is what He is doing right now—holding all things together. There is not a situation or circumstance we will ever encounter that will surprise Him. Everything we face has first passed through His hand. When we face trials or loss, He is already at work with a plan to redeem our stories.

Let's look again at the ceremonial cornerstone and ask the hard question: Is Jesus a cosmetic, ceremonial stone in my life? Have I put Him in a position where I wear "Jesus" like a name tag that affects nothing (or very little) about my life? Sure, the label might affect my schedule on the weekend or a few moments a day when I'm supposed to be praying or reading my Bible, but does it actually have an impact on the way I'm living?

If we wear His name, it should affect *absolutely everything*. He should be in every scenario and situation and every relationship. He is present in every fear you have, every hope you have, every dream.

I would guess many claim to be Christians and only have a ceremonial cornerstone in Jesus. They don't know what it means to put Jesus in the chief cornerstone position in their life. I think this is like a person who wears a team sweatshirt just as a convenient garment. They know nothing about who plays for the team and have never been to a game. They may not even root for this team. They just got a really great clearance deal on a hoodie at Target.

What would your life look like without Jesus? Would it crumble? Would you even notice if He was missing? Is He King of your life or just a convenient cosmetic piece of outerwear? Peter told the religious leaders that "Jesus is 'the stone you builders rejected, which has become the cornerstone.' Salvation is found in no one else, for there is no other name under heaven given to mankind by which we must be saved" (Acts 4:11–12). There is nothing else worthy of that position in our lives.

When we look at the invitation to build our lives on Christ as the cornerstone, we can have a tendency to get a little inward focused. We look at where we've missed the mark and how we've not built well. But when we look at Ephesians 2, we see we've been made fellow citizens anyway. We are members of God's household. We are His people. Even when we've chosen our own way and we've set a cornerstone other than Christ, God still says we can come home. We belong at His table. We are welcome. We are members of His household, part of His building, a dwelling place for God Himself, and we receive everything that goes along with that position.

First Peter 2:4–6 tells us, "As you come to him, the living Stone—rejected by humans but chosen by God and precious to him—you also, like living stones, are being built into a spiritual house to be a holy priesthood, offering spiritual sacrifices acceptable to God through Jesus Christ. For in Scripture it says: 'See, I lay a stone in Zion, a chosen and precious cornerstone, and the one who trusts in him will never be put to shame.'" We are living stones. We are being built into spiritual houses for the glory of our God. Christ is the foundation and we are the stones. When we choose Him, we will never be covered with shame. Jesus will not fail us. Things may not turn out the way we think they should or the way we hoped they would or the way we wished they would, but God will *never* fail us.

When we do choose Christ as the cornerstone, we can live without having to be in control. When we remember who Jesus is, our fears don't rule the day.

Maybe you're tired of holding it all together. Maybe your foundation is crumbling a little and you need something to change. Jesus says, "Can you let Me be the thing everything rests on? Can you allow Me to be the One who holds it all together?" The best answer to those questions is a resounding yes!

Rebuilding is hard work, but Jesus is a master builder. May He give us a glimpse of life with a new foundation and the courage to step into the reconstruction process with Him. Jesus, renovate us.

LISTEN AND LINGER

Read through Ephesians 1:18–23; 2:19–22; and 1 Peter 2:4–6.

Which cornerstone definition resonates the most with you right now?

What other "hopes" have you placed in the cornerstone position?

How have those failed you or how could you see them failing you?

What is different about placing Jesus in the cornerstone position?

IDENTIFY YOUR CORNERSTONE

It's one of my favorite sounds in the world. I love to hear the bride of Christ singing His praise with resounding voices. As a worship leader, I'm struck at times by how easily I can allow words to cross my lips without even considering what they might mean if I *really* lived them. I recognize there are situations when we sing what we hope to be—casting a vision, of sorts.

It's easy to allow the words to slip out without a thought. We croon, "Christ alone, Cornerstone," yet, when we begin to peel back the layers, seeing what's underneath, can we really say this is true? Is our hope built on nothing less, nothing more than Jesus?

I know at various times in my life, I've placed my hope in other things. Things like my own ability to perform or the opinions of others. A job opportunity or having a certain amount of money in the bank. Another person holding up their end of an agreement or a scheduled plan working a precise way to provide a specific and certain outcome. I'm not proud of it, but it's been an issue—placing my hope in these other things.

You know what? Every single time, these things fell short. They missed the mark. They didn't deliver. When they crashed, other things crumbled along with them.

Not so with Jesus.

Every time I've put my hope in Him, He's been faithful. He's delivered. It's not always been what I anticipated or at times even hoped for, but He's done His part. I've *never* been disappointed by Him. Sure, I've been disappointed because the outcome hasn't been what I wanted or expected. But Jesus? He's never let me down.

As we learned about the cornerstone, I've been convicted to examine myself to see how this foundational block is demonstrated in my own life. Here's a refresher:

Cornerstone or "foundation" stone: the first stone set; the basic element on which all else depends

Ceremonial cornerstone: a block that has no bearing on the foundation and is only cosmetic in nature

As you read these definitions, which type of cornerstone would you apply to your relationship with Christ?

How do you see that description playing out in your regular life?

Have you chosen the ceremonial stone at times, wearing the name "Christian," but not giving Jesus the rightful place as the first stone set, influencing all the other stones?

Isaiah 28:16 tells us about our cornerstone:

So this is what the Sovereign LORD says:

> "See, I lay a stone in Zion, a tested stone,
> a precious cornerstone for a sure foundation;
> the one who relies on it
> will never be stricken with panic."

Jesus was this stone, the tested stone, the Sovereign Lord referred to in this passage.

When in your life have you known Jesus to be a sure foundation?

When has your panic subsided because He is the one on whom you rely?

In your own Bible, read through Ephesians 1:18–23 and 2:18–22 with the different "cornerstone" explanations in mind.

What stands out in these passages as you think about Jesus as the cornerstone?

How is God inviting you to live differently as a result?

Lord Jesus, teach me what it looks like to make You a true cornerstone in my life. Reveal to me where I have made You simply a ceremonial cornerstone, bearing Your name, but not allowing You to determine anything else in my life. Forgive me for those times. Help me to surrender to You. You are worth it and You are faithful. You will never disappoint or fail me. Thank You for that truth. Help me to believe it and live what I know is true. Amen.

My Prayer:

Journaling Prompt:

What would it look like to allow Christ to determine how your house (life) should be built, to allow everything to rest on Him? What would be the same? What would be different?

REJECTED CORNERSTONE

It's a word we're all familiar with, and probably have negative feelings rise up within us when we even hear it: *rejection*. No one likes rejection. It stings. It wounds. It crushes. We don't like to be the object of someone's rejection. Yet, it's something that happens to all of us.

Being on the other side of rejection, however, certainly doesn't feel quite the same way, does it? When we're the ones doling it out, it's a bit different than being the recipient.

The dictionary defines "reject" this way:

1. *To refuse to have, take, recognize, etc.*

2. *To refuse to accept (someone or something); rebuff.*

3. *To discard as useless or unsatisfactory.*

4. *To cast out or off.*[18]

If I asked you if you had ever rejected Jesus, what would you say? Maybe you could point to a specific time in your life when you did just that—when you walked away or you flat-out denied Him. But I'm guessing in your story, like mine, the rejection is probably a bit more subtle.

I'm thinking it's possible at times you've rejected Jesus as your ultimate cornerstone. Maybe when you just wanted your own way or when you've not wanted Jesus to have that much authority in your life. You know, determining everything you do like a *real* cornerstone does.

---

18. Reject. Dictionary.com. *Dictionary.com Unabridged.* Random House, Inc. http://www.dictionary.com/browse/reject?s=t.

I've been guilty of that so many times. Guilty of refusing to recognize the path Jesus wants me to take. Refusing to accept His best for my life. Discarding His truth as merely a suggestion instead of a life-giving promise. I've been guilty of casting Him off.

But at other times, I have chosen Him. I have put Him first. I've given Him the rightful privilege of determining my steps and charting my course. It's not always easy and I don't always choose it, but when I do, it's beautiful and breathes so much life into me!

Today we're going to spend some time with Peter and John before the Sanhedrin. Peter and John's audience was highly religious, holding to the law at all costs. They thought they knew it all. (Sounds a little like us sometimes, huh?)

Read Acts 4:1–22 in your own Bible.

Now begin to imagine the scene as if you were right in the middle of it.

What do you see?

What do you hear?

What do you smell?

What's your position?

Who else is there with you?

What are you feeling?

What's the mood of the group?

What do you think of all of this?

What questions do you have?

Don't worry about historical accuracy. Just allow God to bring the story to life. Remember, these people we read about in Scripture were real people who walked the earth and had feelings and thoughts much like ours.

Write down some of the major things you notice. Again, don't worry about historical accuracy. Just allow God to bring the story to life.

What are your observations about the text? What is God calling you to do as a result of this passage?

Lord Jesus, thank You that You are indeed the cornerstone whether I, or anyone else, rejects You. Your place on the throne is not determined by what I think or how I act. You are sovereign anyway. Thank You for that truth. Help me to believe it and live what I know is true. Amen.

My Prayer:

Journaling Prompt:

How have you at times rejected Jesus as the cornerstone? When have you chosen Him? What has been the difference? What is God inviting you into right now as a result of reading this passage?

POWERFUL CORNERSTONE

It was an unusual morning for us. I think spring fever had set in and the sun was finally shining, making us a bit giddy. Abigail and I were waiting for her school bus to arrive. We were talking, laughing, and listening to some crazy music that may or may not have led to a dance party at the end of the driveway. (This is not a typical morning for us. Most of the time there is some form of prodding and possibly some elevated speech that ensues while getting ready for the day, but I can't be certain.)

We were enjoying the wait when at the same moment, we both noticed the sky. It was remarkable. Stunning. Layers of turquoise, magenta, deep oranges, bright yellow, and powder blue. The sky burst with colors and clouds. It was as if God painted a spectacular "Good morning" in the heavens just for the two of us.

He tells the ocean where to stop. He put the stars in their places in the sky, making pictures with them. He commands and controls the weather—the wind and the rain, thunder, lightning. The sky is His canvas, His palette filled with unlimited hues. He brushes the sky with colors that make you stop breathing for a moment. He's *that* powerful. Our cornerstone isn't just another guy. *He's the Creator and Sustainer of the entire universe.* There is nothing that has been created that He did not make.

Let's see what Isaiah 40 has to say about our powerful cornerstone. We're going to use the Listen, Linger, Learn, and Live method to encounter this text today.

LISTEN

Read through Isaiah 40:10–26 in your own Bible. Sit quietly for a moment before you begin. Ask the Holy Spirit to speak and show you what the Lord wants for you in this passage. Mark words or phrases in your Bible that stand out as you read.

LINGER

Read the passage again out loud. Are the same words or phrases you marked the first time still standing out? Write them below. How do these words or phrases apply to your life right now?

LEARN

As you read the text for the third time, ask yourself, How is God inviting me to respond? What does He want me to be learning from this? What am I noticing? Write out what comes to mind.

LIVE

Read the passage one last time and answer these questions:

Why is God showing me this now?

What does this mean for my life?

How do I need to live differently?

How do I need to respond to God's invitation?

Lord Jesus, You are the all-powerful, Mighty God. I so often forget the power You hold. Remind me that nothing can contain You. Remind me that You do not take advice from anyone. Even though I cannot possibly understand how powerful You truly are, I know You are sovereign and in control. Thank You for that truth. Help me to believe it and live what I know is true. Amen.

My Prayer:

Journaling Prompt:

How does knowing Jesus is all-powerful help you trust Him as your cornerstone? What surprises did you discover in the Isaiah 40 text from today? What invitations is God extending to you in this moment?

WEEK 3 | DAY 4

VICTORIOUS CORNERSTONE

Winners and losers. We learn about them at an early age, don't we? Whether it's a highly anticipated, widely viewed sporting event with a favorite team, or cheering on our kids at the local soccer field or swim meet. Maybe it's awaiting results from an anxiety-inducing political season or landing a role on the church committee. We find winners and losers everywhere. We all like to win. At least I don't know that I've ever met anyone who would rather lose. Of course, we're all taught it is polite to be a gracious loser, but liking it is another story. Let's face it—victory is just sweet.

Do you know that if you're with Jesus, you're on the winning team? Do you realize that in the end God wins? Jesus was, is, and will always be the Victor. He conquered sin and defeated death and we get to reap the benefits. This champion King fights for us and He is a sure thing. Not only is He a powerful cornerstone, He's victorious as well.

Today we're going to dig into a couple of Scriptures where we discover the extent of Christ's conquering reach. I pray you'll begin to understand a little of how His victory impacts us. It's significant. It's something worth building your life upon. Our Jesus is a victorious cornerstone. Using the Bible study SOAP method, let's dive in!

S for Scripture:
Read slowly through the Scriptures below. Mark in the texts truths you discover about Jesus.

> What I am saying, dear brothers and sisters, is that our physical bodies cannot inherit the kingdom of God. These dying bodies cannot inherit what will last forever.

But let me reveal to you a wonderful secret. We will not all die, but we will all be transformed! It will happen in a moment, in the blink of an eye, when the last trumpet is blown. For when the trumpet sounds, those who have died will be raised to live forever. And we who are living will also be transformed. For our dying bodies must be transformed into bodies that will never die; our mortal bodies must be transformed into immortal bodies.

Then, when our dying bodies have been transformed into bodies that will never die, this Scripture will be fulfilled:

"Death is swallowed up in victory.
O death, where is your victory?
O death, where is your sting?"

For sin is the sting that results in death, and the law gives sin its power. But thank God! He gives us victory over sin and death through our Lord Jesus Christ.

So, my dear brothers and sisters, be strong and immovable. Always work enthusiastically for the Lord, for you know that nothing you do for the Lord is ever useless. (1 Cor. 15:51–58 NLT)

*   *   *

When I turned to see who was speaking to me, I saw seven gold lampstands. And standing in the middle of the lampstands was someone like the Son of Man. He was wearing a long robe with a gold sash across his chest. His head and his hair were white like wool, as white as snow. And his eyes were like flames of fire. His feet were like polished bronze refined in a furnace, and his voice thundered like mighty ocean waves. He held seven stars in his right hand, and a sharp two-edged sword came from his mouth. And his face was like the sun in all its brilliance.

When I saw him, I fell at his feet as if I were dead. But he laid his right hand on me and said, "Don't be afraid! I am the First and the Last. I am the living one. I died, but look—I am alive forever and ever! And I hold the keys of death and the grave. (Rev. 1:12–18 NLT)

O for Observation:

What do you notice in what you marked? Do you believe these things to be true about God? What are your other observations about the text? What stands out?

A for Application:

How is God calling you to apply the truth in this Scripture to your life right now? What is He calling you to change? How is He inviting you to be different?

P for Prayer:

PRAYER FOR THE DAY

Lord Jesus, You are victorious! I'm not always quick to believe it or to remember that it's true, but it is. Help me in my times of unbelief or really just my negligence to recall Your story of triumph. You have indeed defeated death and conquered sin on my behalf. Thank You for that truth. Help me to believe it and live what I know is true. Amen.

My Prayer:

What can you pray as a result of what God is calling you to do in this passage? What do you need to praise God for, confess to God, or request of Him in response?

Journaling Prompt:

What would be different in your life if you believed Jesus was a victorious cornerstone? How would this affect your everyday, ordinary life?

MY FOUNDATION

Junior church. The place with the cold, metal folding chairs in the unadorned basement. The training ground for disciples. We learned all kinds of songs, watched stories come to life on felt boards with two-dimensional Jesus cutouts, made a game of Bible drills, and occasionally ate donuts.

One of the songs I distinctly remember had hand motions (as most songs in junior church did) and a catchy little refrain. "The rains came down and the floods came up. The rains came down and the floods came up. The rains came down and the floods came up, and the house on the sand went *splat!*"

Splat. I've experienced this with my own life before. Storms will come. Life will be hard. Splatting happens. But it doesn't have to. We can't calm the storms and we definitely will not be exempt from them. They can't be contained or controlled by our efforts. What we can control, however, is the kind of foundation our lives are built on. We can choose sandy, loose, unreliable ground for our foundation. Or we can choose solid, immovable, unshakeable rock as our cornerstone.

Today we're going to look at the parable in this children's song. We'll look at the passage in four different versions in two gospels using the Listen, Linger, Learn, and Live Bible study method. Jesus calls one of the builders wise and the other foolish. I've sure spent my fair share of time being foolish. At the end of the day, though, I want to be wise. I want to build my life on the things that matter—the person who will withstand any storm that comes my way because the winds and waves obey His voice.

LISTEN

Read through Luke 6:46–49 in the NIV. Sit quietly for a moment before you begin. Ask the Holy Spirit to speak and show you what the Lord wants for you in this passage. Mark words or phrases that stand out as you read.

"Why do you call me, 'Lord, Lord,' and do not do what I say? As for everyone who comes to me and hears my words and puts them into practice, I will show you what they are like. They are like a man building a house, who dug down deep and laid the foundation on rock. When a flood came, the torrent struck that house but could not shake it, because it was well built. But the one who hears my words and does not put them into practice is like a man who built a house on the ground without a foundation. The moment the torrent struck that house, it collapsed and its destruction was complete."

LINGER

Read the passage again out loud in The Message version. Are the same words or phrases you marked the first time still standing out? Write them down. How do these words or phrases apply to your life right now?

"Why are you so polite with me, always saying 'Yes, sir,' and 'That's right, sir,' but never doing a thing I tell you? These words I speak to you are not mere additions to your life, homeowner improvements to your standard of living. They are foundation words, words to build a life on.

If you work the words into your life, you are like a smart carpenter who dug deep and laid the foundation of his house on bedrock. When the river burst its banks and crashed against the house, nothing could shake it; it was built to last. But if you just use my words in Bible studies and don't work them into your life, you are like a dumb carpenter who built a house but skipped the foundation. When the swollen river came crashing in, it collapsed like a house of cards. It was a total loss."

As you read the narrative for the third time (this time in Matthew 7:24–27 in the New Living Translation), ask yourself, "How is God inviting me to respond? What does He want me to be learning from this? What am I noticing?" Write out what comes to mind.

> "Anyone who listens to my teaching and follows it is wise, like a person who builds a house on solid rock. Though the rain comes in torrents and the floodwaters rise and the winds beat against that house, it won't collapse because it is built on bedrock. But anyone who hears my teaching and doesn't obey it is foolish, like a person who builds a house on sand. When the rains and floods come and the winds beat against that house, it will collapse with a mighty crash."

LIVE

Read the Matthew passage one last time in The Voice[19] and answer these questions:

Why is God showing me this now?

What does this mean for my life?

How do I need to live differently?

How do I need to respond to God's invitation?

"Those people who are listening to Me, those people who hear what I say and live according to My teachings—you are like a wise man who built his house on a rock, on a firm foundation. When storms hit, rain pounded down and waters rose, levees broke and winds beat all the walls of that house. But the house did not fall because it was built upon rock. Those of you who are listening and do not hear—you are like a fool who builds a house on sand. When a storm comes to his house, what will happen? The rain will fall, the waters will rise, the wind will blow, and his house will collapse with a great crash."

PRAYER FOR THE DAY

Lord Jesus, reveal to me where my foundation is shaky. Show me where I have built my life on something other than You. Give me the courage to uproot those places and allow You to rebuild them. You are strong and can weather any storm that may come. Thank You for that truth. Help me to believe it and live what I know is true. Amen.

My Prayer:

Journaling Prompt:

What type of cornerstone and foundation do you really have? Is it strong enough to withstand a powerful storm? What storms in your life have revealed your foundation?

WEEK THREE: REFLECT AND ACT

The cornerstone matters. And you are currently embracing one type of corner-stone. You may even be like me and just switch back and forth on occasion. Either way, we've made a choice whether we realize it or not.

Is Jesus just a badge you wear? A name you claim, but doesn't really affect the way you live your life? A ceremonial cornerstone?

Or is He setting the course of every life decision because He has been set as *the* cornerstone for your life? And like the keystone, is everything resting on Jesus in your life? Is it He you depend on to hold it all together? Let's take some space to reflect on what you've learned this week.

Take some time to answer each of these questions in your journal:

What new truths did God reveal through my time in His Word this week?

What challenged me?

What am I still struggling to believe?

What are God's invitations to me right now?

Are there themes or patterns in what God is showing me? If so, what are they?

What action steps do I need to follow as a result of what I've learned this week?

Christ alone.

He's the *only* Cornerstone that can hold all things together. Every time.

O, God of My Future:

Today, I dive into waters, unknown.

The sudden embrace of its cold startles me, awakens hiding fear.

I do not know about the next, or how it may be cruel.

I need your help, God.

To trust more than I doubt.

Rest more than wrestle.

I am afraid of the future. And yet, You are already there.

I live in the unknown. And yet, You live with me.

I want to dance where I now sit, scared, in corners.

I want You to see me, know who I am,

　　recognize my inability to be anything but rattling bones

　　without You.

I need strength. I need hope. I need promises. I need safety.

More than anything, I need to be able to face what I do not know

　　with courage I do not have.

This, God, will only come from You.

So help me not be scared.

Give me eyes to see beyond the natural.

And when my flesh threatens to pull me under in the waters of

fear, come with strong hands to bring me back to life.

Amen.[20]

—LISA WHITTLE

20. "O, God of My Future" from "Prayer for the Unknown," www.lisawhittle.com, April 3, 2014. Used with permission.

our eyes are on You

"If calamity comes upon us, whether the sword of judgment, or plague or famine, we will stand in your presence before this temple that bears your Name and will cry out to you in our distress, and you will hear us and save us." 2 CHRONICLES 20:9

A great king faces a great battle. A time of peace interrupted by a raging war. Facing an unknown outcome, the people of Judah approach their known God, begging Him to deliver them.

This week we have the privilege of digging into a powerful story of how King Jehoshaphat navigated a very difficult situation when he couldn't see the outcome. The story we're dwelling on this week is flooded with beautiful nuances that I hope you will allow to really sink in.

Our stories are not much different from this great king's. We are staring into the unknown, facing giants and enemies too powerful for us. They press in on all sides. Will we choose, like Jehoshaphat, to surrender to the Sovereign Lord? I'm praying you will allow the Holy Spirit to reveal how your story intersects with this one.

We're going to spend some time lingering in the same text for most of the week. Don't be discouraged by the repetition. Allow God to meet you in it. I'm positive He'll show you something new each day if you let Him. His Word is powerful that way.

Let's dig in and learn from one of my favorite stories in the Old Testament!

My prayer for us this week:

Lord Jesus,
Help us to keep our eyes on You. It's hard when we face big things to remember You are in control. Help us to anchor ourselves in Your Word and in worship. Help us, like King Jehoshaphat, to rely on You and You alone. You are strong enough to save us.
Amen.

INTRODUCTION TO WEEK 4
OUR EYES ARE ON YOU

I broke my favorite frosty mug this morning. It shattered on the garage floor. (Please don't ask why I had a frosty mug of milk in my garage. And please don't judge either.) Milk splattered all over the floor, my feet, the rug. But worse than that, my favorite frosty mug is gone.

I know this seems like a trite thing, but it felt really big . . . because this week has been filled with hard things, heavy things swirling through my mind and weighing on my heart. It really wasn't about the mug.

Here's what we need to remember: a war is raging. A battle has been waged for your soul and for mine. We have an enemy, relentless in his pursuit, whose only desire is to devour and destroy us (1 Peter 5:8). He uses any means necessary. Even a smashed mug.

It might be that your life is just moving right along without a hitch. If so, that's wonderful! If that is the case, there is still a war going on for custody of your soul. The beautiful truth is, however, if you belong to Christ, you're already on the winning side![21] If you don't feel the effects of the battle, they will surface and I want you to be ready.

If you feel like you are standing on the war-torn battleground, wounded and weary, please know there is hope. God sees you and He's at work behind the scenes fighting for you every step of the way.

Wherever you are on the battlefield, 2 Chronicles 20:1–30 teaches us a great deal about how to face a raging war in a godly way. King Jehoshaphat's approach to war anchored the people of Judah at a pivotal time. We're going to walk through these verses this week and glean all we can for fighting our own battles. Let's take a look at what Jehoshaphat has to teach us.

---

21. If you have never surrendered to Christ, He wants to be in a relationship with you. Romans 8 tells us "there is now no condemnation for those who are in Christ Jesus." In order to be a part of the winning side, you must belong to Christ. In order to belong to Christ, we must confess Jesus as Lord and believe He is the Son of God. Then it is important for us to also be obedient to Him in baptism. If you are not yet a follower of Christ and need to choose Him, please take time to talk to someone about this very important decision. Christ is the bridge, but you must accept Him before you can walk across. He is waiting for you—waiting to show grace, mercy, and love.

Jehoshaphat's father, King Asa, was not a great role model. He had a good beginning (2 Chron. 14:1–15), but it didn't take long for that to change. He trusted himself and his alliances more than he trusted the almighty God. At times, he relied on God and other times, he just didn't (2 Chron. 16:7–9). Asa tried to fix things on his own instead of allowing God to fight for them. As a result, for the remainder of Asa's reign, the nation of Judah experienced war.

Asa didn't finish well, but Jehoshaphat learned from his father's mistakes. When he became king, he chose to walk with God as his forefather David had done, a man after God's own heart (2 Chron. 17:1–3; 1 Sam. 13:14; Acts 13:22).

> The LORD was with Jehoshaphat because he followed the ways of his father David before him. He did not consult the Baals but sought the God of his father and followed his commands rather than the practices of Israel. The LORD established the kingdom under his control; and all Judah brought gifts to Jehoshaphat, so that he had great wealth and honor. His heart was devoted to the ways of the LORD; furthermore, he removed the high places and the Asherah poles from Judah.
>
> In the third year of his reign he sent his officials . . . to teach in the towns of Judah. With them were certain Levites . . . and the priests Elishama and Jehoram. They taught throughout Judah, taking with them the Book of the Law of the LORD; they went around to all the towns of Judah and taught the people.
>
> The fear of the LORD fell on all the kingdoms of the lands surrounding Judah, so that they did not go to war against Jehoshaphat. (2 Chron. 17:3–10)

The almighty God poured His favor over King Jehoshaphat as a result of his choices. He turned the nation of Judah back to God. He sent out the Levite priests along with the officials to teach the book of the Law—God's Word. He gathered the people and laid a foundation of the Word of God.

God responded by allowing the fear of the Lord to fall on all the surrounding kingdoms, which in turn brought a time of peace to Judah after a time of perpetual battle. The people of Judah experienced protection and prospered in this season of peace, and Jehoshaphat became more and more powerful. He built forts and cities and received gifts from his terrified neighbors. But they don't just sit around in Judah; Jehoshaphat keeps his men trained for battle just in case (2 Chron. 17:12–19).

During this season of peace, Jehoshaphat made a mistake. He formed an alliance with King Ahab, the king of Israel. Let's just say that King Ahab and King Jehoshaphat did not share a devoted love of God. They went to war together even after the prophet Micaiah foretells King Ahab's death if he does. Ahab tried to outrun the prophecy by wearing a disguise, and he still doesn't make it out alive (2 Chron. 18:1–34).

When Jehoshaphat returned from battle, his advisors told him God was not pleased with his choices. He's faced with the wrongs he's done and the reality that his heart isn't right with God. They reminded him of the good he had done, ridding the land of the idols (2 Chron. 19:1–3). Because Jehoshaphat was indeed a man after God's own heart, he repented, and turned back to God. He went out again among the people and turned their hearts back to the almighty God as well. He reminded them of who God was, what His law said, and how to follow Him (2 Chron. 19:4–10). The last time King Jehoshaphat had turned the people back to God, peace resulted. We see that what follows this time is a bit different.

In the opening words of 2 Chronicles 20, the Moabites, Ammonites, and some Meunites are on their way to make war against Jehoshaphat. It wasn't something that could be negotiated at this point. They were en route, coming to fight the people of Judah. What happened next is remarkable!

> Alarmed, Jehoshaphat resolved to inquire of the Lord, and he proclaimed a fast for all Judah. The people of Judah came together to seek help from the Lord; indeed, they came from every town in Judah to seek him. (2 Chron. 20:3–4)

Of course, Jehoshaphat was alarmed! He had people from three different nations coming for him. But he resolved (made an intentional decision) to inquire of the Lord, proclaiming a fast for all of Judah. He didn't just sit back and fret, "Oh, no, war is coming! Hmmm, I wonder how this is all going to go down?" Instead, he resolved to inquire of God and say, "We need You. Tell me what we need to do." Not only did he seek the Lord himself, but he invited others into the process of prayer and fasting. He called on the entire kingdom to participate in seeking God for an answer to the unknown territory ahead of them.

Remember, there has already been a deposit made in the people of Judah. They know God's Word because Jehoshaphat made sure that in times of peace, they learned about it. They've had it read to them and taught to them on multiple occasions. It's been laid as a foundational groundwork for this moment. They know how God has shown up before, delivering His people over and over again. Seeking God wasn't a new thing just because of impending calamity. This moment awakens something that has already been deposited within them.

Then, in the middle of the assembly, Jehoshaphat offers a bold prayer, petitioning God on behalf of the nation of Judah.

> "LORD, the God of our ancestors, are you not the God who is in heaven? You rule over all the kingdoms of the nations. Power and might are in your hand, and no one can withstand you. Our God, did you not drive out the inhabitants of this land before your people Israel and give it forever to the descendants of Abraham your friend? They have lived in it and have built in it a sanctuary for your Name, saying, 'If calamity comes upon us, whether the sword of judgment, or plague or famine, we will stand in your presence before this temple that bears your Name and will cry out to you in our distress, and you will hear us and save us.'
>
> "But now here are men from Ammon, Moab and Mount Seir, whose territory you would not allow Israel to invade when they came from Egypt; so they turned away from them and did not destroy them. See how

they are repaying us by coming to drive us out of the possession you gave
us as an inheritance. Our God, will you not judge them? For we have no
power to face this vast army that is attacking us. We do not know what to
do, but our eyes are on you." (2 Chron. 20:6–12)

Jehoshaphat begins declaring who God is—this is who we *know* You to be: over all,
all-powerful, in control. This is the God we are asking for help. He addresses God,
not only directing his petition to God Himself, but also proclaiming it for all of
Judah to hear and be reminded. He continues in verses 7–9 announcing what God
has done before, but also confessing Israel's trust and surrender to God's will. He's
essentially saying, "War is coming. If this gets to us, this is what we will do. We will
stand on the steps of Your house and will petition You in Your name and beg You
to show up on our behalf." The people are in distress. They're standing outside the
temple asking God to be their rescue, trusting God will hear them and respond.

In verses 10–11, Jehoshaphat simply tells God their requests. He states the need for
help, telling God the details, asking something very specific of Him. He's reminding God of how they've done what has been asked of them. Jehoshaphat is also
declaring what God gave them in the land. These verses hold the plea for a savior.

Verse 12 contains the ultimate surrender and humility. Jehoshaphat, this great
king of Judah who holds wealth and power, admits his need. He tells God they
are unable to face the vast army coming to attack. Then he says, "We do not know
what to do, but our eyes are upon you."

They will not be able to save themselves. A huge unknown faces Jehoshaphat
and the people of Judah, but they fix their eyes on their Deliverer, the Lord God
Almighty. They were waiting for God to show them what to do.

All the men of Judah, with their wives and children and little ones, stood
there before the Lord. (v. 13)

And that's what they did. They waited on God. They didn't move until they heard from Him. They stood before God, awaiting His plan. Then the Spirit of the Lord spoke through Jahaziel, a priest of the Lord. God answered their prayers with a plan.

> He said: "Listen, King Jehoshaphat and all who live in Judah and Jerusalem! This is what the LORD says to you: 'Do not be afraid or discouraged because of this vast army. For the battle is not yours, but God's. Tomorrow march down against them. They will be climbing up by the Pass of Ziz, and you will find them at the end of the gorge in the Desert of Jeruel. You will not have to fight this battle. Take up your positions; stand firm and see the deliverance the LORD will give you, Judah and Jerusalem. Do not be afraid; do not be discouraged. Go out to face them tomorrow, and the LORD will be with you.'" (vv. 15–17)

Jahaziel declares the battle belongs to God, who then gives instructions through this priest's words, specific instructions on how to win the battle. He basically tells them to march into battle and *stand still*. I'm sure they might be thinking, "So, You just want us to march down there and *stand still*? But we're an ARMY! And You want us to just stand still?" But that's not the response we see.

> Jehoshaphat bowed down with his face to the ground, and all the people of Judah and Jerusalem fell down in worship before the LORD. Then some Levites from the Kohathites and Korahites stood up and praised the LORD, the God of Israel, with a very loud voice. (vv. 18–19)

Their immediate response is to *worship*. They honor God and give Him praise *before* He wins the battle. They praise Him for hearing their prayers and for responding with a plan. They're believing and trusting God to do what He's said He will do.

The day of battle arrives. The atmosphere was charged with excitement of how God would move among them. And likely some trepidation crept in at times. Jehoshaphat gets the army ready.

They start to put God's plan into motion. With one small change: Jehoshaphat appoints worship leaders to the front line. He instructs them to praise the Lord at the head of the pack, singing, "Give thanks to the LORD, for his love endures forever" (vv. 20–21).

This is the only change in the plan God gave, and Jehoshaphat consulted the people before implementing the change rather than make the shift in isolation. Can you envision what people would think if they saw a small marching band in the front of the army singing praises to God? It was probably either a bit laughable or incredibly intimidating!

As they prepare, Jehoshaphat affirms the plan God set in place.

> Early in the morning they left for the Desert of Tekoa. As they set out, Jehoshaphat stood and said, "Listen to me, Judah and people of Jerusalem! Have faith in the LORD your God and you will be upheld; have faith in his prophets and you will be successful." (v. 20)

Jehoshaphat doesn't just tell them they will be successful because he *thinks* so. He believes what God has said He will do, He *will* do. And He does. God does what He says He will do.

> As they began to sing and praise, the LORD set ambushes against the men of Ammon and Moab and Mount Seir who were invading Judah, and they were defeated. The Ammonites and Moabites rose up against the men from Mount Seir to destroy and annihilate them. After they finished slaughtering the men from Seir, they helped to destroy one another.
>
> When the men of Judah came to the place that overlooks the desert and looked toward the vast army, they saw only dead bodies lying on the ground; no one had escaped. (vv. 22–24)

The men of Judah follow God's instructions and God delivers them. Their enemies came together to advance against the people of Judah, but God confused them and they annihilated one another. There were zero survivors. Zero. God allowed this outcome in order to protect His people.

Not only does God obliterate their enemies, but He provides for the people of Judah with plunder. In fact, so much was left that it took them three full days to collect it all. God provided food, clothing, weaponry, articles of value, and more that would sustain them for quite a while. He provided not only for their deliverance but for their needs at the same time.

After three days of collecting loot, what was their response? They responded as they had all along. On the fourth day, they gathered together and worshiped, praising the Lord for His faithfulness (2 Chron. 20:26). Jehoshaphat led the army back to Jerusalem, rejoicing all the way. Their first stop was the temple of the Lord where they continued to praise Him with harps and lyres and trumpets (vv. 27–28). As a result of this victory for the people of Judah, the fear of God came upon the surrounding kingdoms and Judah experienced peace once again. God granted King Jehoshaphat rest on every side (vv. 29–30).

A great story, right? But what does this have to do with us? As we discussed earlier, war is coming in some form. Get ready, because it's on its way.

What will our response be when it does come? Will we resolve to seek the face of God like Jehoshaphat? Will we feast on the book of the Law so we have a strong foundation like the people of Judah? Will we hide God's Word in our heart so we know the God we are actually approaching when we ask for help?

Will we fix our eyes on Jesus, the author and perfecter of our faith (Heb. 12:2)? Will we set our eyes on things above, not on earthly things (Col. 3:2)? Like the psalmist, we can lift our eyes to the hills, knowing our help comes from the Lord, the maker of heaven and earth (Ps. 121:1–2). When we have done these things, it's up to Him to do the rest.

Will we worship *before* we see the results? Will we continue to worship God regardless of the outcome? Sometimes we don't see the victory right away. At times, it can be far off and distant. Will we worship even if calamity comes? Will we choose to believe the promises of God and stand firm on them?

The people of Judah joined together to seek God. The corporate nature of their prayer was significant. The gathered body of Christ, worshiping and waiting on God is a powerful thing. Do we lean on the body of Christ in these moments?

Maybe you're already in the midst of a war. If so, it's not too late to seek the face of God with resolve. If not, there's time to make deposits and build a foundation that will withstand the battle ahead. God's promises are still true. He is fighting for you.

LISTEN AND LINGER

Read 2 Chronicles 20:1–30.

What stands out in this story?

When have you noticed the deposits of God's Word making a difference in your life?

When has worship changed your situation?

What promises of God do you need to remember right now?

FIX YOUR EYES

I may or may not have listened to a lot of Madonna when I was growing up. (Don't judge, please.) I recall the opening of one of her songs vividly. There was a strong chord and a simple phrase stated with quite the attitude, "What are you lookin' at?" Then the string progression and rhythmic hand claps for "Vogue" kicked in. I'm not sure what I thought about when I first heard it or the many times I heard it after, but those words mean something very different to me now.

So much of the time, I'm not even aware of what I'm looking at, where I'm choosing to place my focus. We're told in Hebrews 12:2 to fix our eyes on Jesus, but there have been times in my life when I wasn't exactly sure what that meant. I'm learning more and more what it might be like to fix my eyes on Jesus as I walk with Him.

The Greek word for "fixing" in this text means to turn the eyes away from other things and fix them on something;[22] to fix one's attention on;[23] to consider attentively.[24] In other words, it's a deliberate act. It's not something that happens by chance. It takes effort and intentionality.

Similarly, in Colossians 3:2, we're told to "set our minds on things above, not on earthly things." The Greek word for "set" here means "to exercise the mind, to be disposed in a certain direction; to interest oneself in; to set the affection on; to be of the same mind."[25] Again, not something that will happen by accident. I've never known any exercise to happen by accident. We have to do the directing, the disposing, the setting of the affection in order to see the result of living this way.

Jehoshaphat knew something about fixing his eyes on God—especially in difficult circumstances. Today we're going to take a look at the opening part of this week's story through the lens of Hebrews 12:2 and Colossians 3:2.

22. Robert L. Thomas, *New American Standard Hebrew-Aramaic and Greek Dictionaries: Updated Edition* (Anaheim, CA: Foundation Publications, Inc., 1998).
23. James Swanson, *Dictionary of Biblical Languages with Semantic Domains: Greek (New Testament)* (Oak Harbor, WA: Logos Research Systems, Inc., 1997).
24. James Strong, *A Concise Dictionary of the Words in the Greek Testament and The Hebrew Bible* (Bellingham, WA: Logos Bible Software, 2009).
25. Strong, *A Concise Dictionary*.

Before you read today's main text, write out Hebrews 12:2 and Colossians 3:2 in the space below. Mark words or phrases that stand out in each passage.

With these texts in mind, use the SOAP method to study 2 Chronicles 20:1–12.

S for Scripture:
Read slowly through this passage. Mark in the text truths you discover about God.

After this, the Moabites and Ammonites with some of the Meunites came to wage war against Jehoshaphat.

Some people came and told Jehoshaphat, "A vast army is coming against you from Edom, from the other side of the Dead Sea. It is already in Hazezon Tamar" (that is, En Gedi). Alarmed, Jehoshaphat resolved to inquire of the LORD, and he proclaimed a fast for all Judah. The people of Judah came together to seek help from the LORD; indeed, they came from every town in Judah to seek him.

Then Jehoshaphat stood up in the assembly of Judah and Jerusalem at the temple of the LORD in the front of the new courtyard and said: "LORD, the God of our ancestors, are you not the God who is in heaven? You rule over all the kingdoms of the nations. Power and might are in your hand, and no one can withstand you. Our God, did you not drive out the inhabitants of this land before your people Israel and give it forever to the descendants of Abraham your friend? They have lived in it and have built in it a sanctuary for your Name, saying, 'If calamity comes upon us, whether the sword of judgment, or plague or famine, we will stand in your presence before this temple that bears your Name and will cry out to you in our distress, and you will hear us and save us.'

"But now here are men from Ammon, Moab and Mount Seir, whose territory you would not allow Israel to invade when they came from Egypt; so they turned away from them and did not destroy them. See how they are repaying us by coming to drive us out of the possession you gave us as an inheritance. Our God, will you not judge them? For we have no power to face this vast army that is attacking us. We do not know what to do, but our eyes are on you."

What do you notice about what you marked? Do you believe these things to be true about God?

O for Observation:

What are your observations about the text? What do you notice? What stands out?

A for Application:

How is God calling you to apply the truth in this Scripture to your life right now? What is He calling you to change? How is He inviting you to be different?

P for Prayer:

Lord Jesus, I long to fix my eyes on You, to set my mind on things above, not on earthly things. Will You show me how to do that? Will You teach me what it means to focus my attention on You? Point out to me when I'm falling short and give me the strength to carry out what You're asking of me. You are enough. You are worth fixing my eyes upon. Thank You for that truth. Help me to believe it and live what I know is true. Amen.

My Prayer:

What can you pray as a result of what God is calling you to do in this passage? What do you need to praise God for, confess to God, or request of Him in response?

Journaling Prompt:

Are you fixing your eyes on Jesus? What difference would it make (or does it make) if (when) you fix your eyes on Jesus?

PRAYER CHANGES THINGS

I'm sure if you've been around the church for any length of time, you've seen something depicting the phrase "Prayer changes things," perhaps on some cute Instagram post or on a plate of some kind.

As corny as it sounds, prayer actually does change things. It changes more than we think, though. Sure, prayer can move the heart of God to action, but more importantly, prayer changes us from the inside out.

In *My Utmost for His Highest*, Oswald Chambers puts it this way:

> It is not so true that "prayer changes things" as that prayer changes *me* and I change things. God has so constituted things that prayer on the basis of Redemption alters the way in which a man looks at things. Prayer is not a question of altering things externally, but of working wonders in a man's disposition.[26]

Through prayer, we discover more of who God is. We cultivate surrender to God's will. We are reminded of the places and spaces where God has shown up in the past. Prayer doesn't always change our circumstances, but it definitely changes the way we view and interact with them. It changes us.

Today we're going to spend some time walking through Jehoshaphat's prayer found in 2 Chronicles 20:5–12, using the New Living Translation. Read through the passage slowly and then respond to each section by writing your own prayer to Jesus.

> Jehoshaphat stood before the community of Judah and Jerusalem in front of the new courtyard at the Temple of the LORD. He prayed, "O LORD, God of our ancestors, you alone are the God who is in heaven. You are

---

26. Oswald Chambers, *My Utmost for His Highest: Selections for the Year* (Grand Rapids, MI: Oswald Chambers Publications; Marshall Pickering, 1986), August 28 selection.

ruler of all the kingdoms of the earth. You are powerful and mighty; no one can stand against you!" (vv. 5–6)

Jehoshaphat begins his prayer by praising God for His mighty power.
Write a prayer of praise addressing God for who He is:

"O our God, did you not drive out those who lived in this land when your people Israel arrived? And did you not give this land forever to the descendants of your friend Abraham? Your people settled here and built this Temple to honor your name." (vv. 7–8)

Jehoshaphat continues his prayer by recalling various things God has done.
Continue your prayer by recounting the wonderful things God has done in your life. Where has He shown up? What have you seen Him do? Write a prayer of gratitude for the ways He has worked on your behalf.

They said, "Whenever we are faced with any calamity such as war, plague, or famine, we can come to stand in your presence before this Temple where your name is honored. We can cry out to you to save us, and you will hear us and rescue us." (v. 9)

Jehoshaphat prays a powerful prayer of surrender to God's will. He confesses his trust in God's sovereignty.

Write your own prayer, surrendering to God's will despite the outcome. Can you say "even if" regardless of what may come? If not, ask for God's help in surrendering.

"And now see what the armies of Ammon, Moab, and Mount Seir are doing. You would not let our ancestors invade those nations when Israel left Egypt, so they went around them and did not destroy them. Now see how they reward us! For they have come to throw us out of your land, which you gave us as an inheritance." (vv. 10–11)

Jehoshaphat spent some time pouring out his complaint before God. He tells God what's going on.

What's going on in your life that you need to convey to God? Take a moment and write out a prayer letting Him know your concerns.

"O our God, won't you stop them? We are powerless against this mighty army that is about to attack us. We do not know what to do, but we are looking to you for help." (v. 12)

Jehoshaphat pleads with God to deliver Judah. He recognizes his own weakness and begs God to do something. He declares they don't know what to do or where to turn, but they are sticking with the Lord.

Write your own prayer asking God for what you need in this moment with whatever obstacles you're facing.

Father God, help me to remember prayer does actually change things. Show me where it's changing me from the inside out. Help me to make prayer my first choice as a weapon and not a last resort. My circumstances, my response within them—these are affected by prayer. You listen to me. You hear me. Thank You for those truths. Help me to believe them and live what I know is true. Amen.

Journaling Prompt:

How does your prayer life differ from Jehoshaphat's prayer? What will it take for you to surrender fully to the Lord? How has prayer changed you?

WORSHIP MATTERS

Perspectives can be difficult to change. Shifting our focus takes effort at times. If I'm honest, there are moments when I don't really have the effort it requires to alter my mindset on my own. I definitely don't always *feel* like changing my perspective. But at certain times, an attention adjustment is exactly what I need.

Yesterday we discovered how prayer changes things within us. Another spiritual practice has a similar effect: worship. When we truly worship, it is impossible for our eyes to *not* be fixed on Jesus. When we choose to honor God and sing His praises, remembering the works of His hands throughout time, there's not a lot of room for other thoughts to occupy our minds. Our circumstances don't change instantly, but our hearts turn to the living God for what we need in those moments.

I love how, in today's text, Jehoshaphat chose to worship not only before the battle, but during it as well. In the middle of the unknown, he sends the worship leaders first. Before they saw any victory at all, they stood on the promises of God, proclaiming them all the way.

My favorite way to define *worship* is our response to God's revelation of who He is and what He has done. God reveals Himself to us and we respond. He shows His nature and character (who He is) through the works of His hands (what He has done). Those truths do not change regardless of our circumstances.

Worship is our first defense. Jehoshaphat knew this reality. He trusted it to be true. Their worship mattered. It matters for us as well. Let's see what the Holy Spirit has to say to us through our text today.

LISTEN

Read through 2 Chronicles 20:1–21 in your own Bible. Sit quietly for a moment before you begin. Ask the Holy Spirit to speak and show you what the Lord wants for you in this passage. Mark words or phrases in your Bible that stand out as you read.

LINGER

Read the passage again out loud. Are the same words or phrases you marked the first time still standing out? Write them in the space below. How do these words or phrases apply to your life right now?

LEARN

As you read the text for the third time, ask yourself, "How is God inviting me to respond? What does He want me to be learning from this? What am I noticing?" Write out what comes to mind.

LIVE

Read the passage one last time and answer these questions:

Why is God showing me this now?

What does this mean for my life?

How do I need to live differently?

How do I need to respond to God's invitation?

PRAYER FOR THE DAY

Almighty God, worshiping You matters. It redirects my thoughts and reminds me of who You truly are. Help me to seek Your face when my circumstances become too difficult to bear. You are in the middle of even the most difficult situations and You are always good. Thank You for that truth. Help me to believe it and live what I know is true. Amen.

My Prayer:

Journaling Prompt:
How have you seen worship change your circumstances in the past? How do you see it in the text you read today? What changes for you knowing worship can be your first defense? What can you praise God for right now in spite of your circumstances?

WEEK 4 | DAY 4

GOD SHOWS UP

Several years ago, our worship team started praying for God to show up. We'd been praying that for a long time. After all, if you have a worship service and God doesn't show up, you really don't have a worship service. It's pretty much more of a concert.

Along the way, something changed in the way we prayed. We started asking God to not only show up, but to show *Himself*, even to show *off*. We began asking Him to astound us. I think God loves to show us His power and glory and majesty. His provision beyond our wildest imagination. He loves to do the remarkable among us, to show immeasurably more than all we could ever ask or imagine (Eph. 3:20).

Those beautiful painted skies when He whispers His grace and new mercies that rise with the sun are for us. The perfectly timed, hope-filled words of a trusted friend or even a stranger that change our perspective, helping us see Him moving in our circumstances are for our good. The faithful provision of daily bread when we think we won't have it is God showing up, moving us to trust His promises more. The victory in the battle we thought we were losing shows us His glory, grace, and ultimately His love for us.

As we continue to dig into the story in 2 Chronicles 20, we find God not only showing up to fight the battle for His people and giving them the victory, but going above and beyond to provide for them, reminding them of His character and His nature.

Today, let's put ourselves in the scene. What would it have been like to see this all happen, particularly when we were facing the unknown of a raging war and possibly death as a result? Remembering the context we've already discovered, let's read the rest of the story found in 2 Chronicles 20:13–30.

Read 2 Chronicles 20:13–30 in your own Bible.

Write down some of the major things you notice. What are your observations about the text?

Now begin to imagine the scene as if you were right in the middle of it. Don't worry too much about historical accuracy. Just allow God to bring the story to life. Remember, these people we read about are real people with real emotions and had thoughts and feelings much like ours.

What do you see?

What do you hear?

What do you smell?

What's your position?

Who else is with you?

What are you feeling?

What's the mood of the group?

What do you think of all of this?

What questions do you have?

What fears do you have?

How do you see God showing Himself in this passage?

How do you think that changed the perspective of the people of Judah?

What was their response?

What would your response have been?

What is God calling you to do as a result of this passage?

How is He inviting you to respond?

Heavenly Father, I love when You show up. Grow my awareness of how You work and move. Thank You for the places where You have given me provision beyond my wildest imagination. You are a God who sees and knows and moves. Thank You for that truth. Help me to believe it and live what I know is true. Amen.

My Prayer:

Journaling Prompt:

Where in your life have you seen God show up? Write down those places of remembrance today. Share your story with someone.

MY HELP COMES FROM THE LORD

I remember it clearly. Her little pigtails bouncing, hands squarely on her hips as she announced, "I can do it myself!" I don't know when exactly it started, but with Abigail it was early. She is fiercely independent, so these moments began pretty much as soon as she could talk.

Asking for help can be difficult. We live in a self-sufficient culture, and at times admitting we need help feels a little like failure. When we choose not to ask for help, we are isolated and operate in our own strength, which has never turned out well for me. Maybe you've had a little more luck with it, but it's typically been a bit disastrous on my end.

Can you imagine what the outcome would have been in 2 Chronicles 20 if Jehoshaphat had not resolved in the beginning to seek the Lord's help? If he had tried to fix the situation in his own strength or control the outcome with his own plan? If he had not fixed his eyes on the Lord, I think the outcome would have been gravely different. In fact, many kings of Judah and of Israel did just that and every single time, the conclusion was not in their favor.

It's no different for us. Of course, every scenario does not always turn out rosy. Sometimes we seek God and calamity does come (more about that next week). But even when it does and we've relied on God, He is in the midst of it and holds a plan for redeeming the entire situation. He has never failed to turn something horrific into something beautiful in my life. It takes time and healing, but He never wastes a single hurt.

We've talked this week about setting our minds on things above and fixing our eyes on Him. Focusing on where our help comes from is a fitting ending to this week, I think. I want to share with you one of my favorite psalms, which holds a dear place in my heart.

My grandfather was a faithful, godly man. He was an elder for over forty years in the church where I grew up. For decades he taught a men's Sunday school class every week. He had stacks of commentaries and sincerely modeled what it meant to dig into studying the Word of God. His impact on the faith legacy of our family was significant.

He lived a long, healthy, vibrant life, and when he was nearing the end of his days, Scripture was a comfort to him. God's Word was something he knew well. It had been deposited as a foundation, just like into the people of Judah. We would all take turns reading Scripture to him as he lay in his hospital bed. It was this psalm that was the last one he heard with his earthly ears, and the words that ushered him home. I hope it brings you similar comfort and peace in whatever battle you are facing.

LISTEN

Read through Psalm 121 in the New Living Translation below. Sit quietly for a moment before you begin. Ask the Holy Spirit to speak and show you what the Lord wants for you in this passage. Mark words or phrases that stand out as you read.

> I look up to the mountains—
>   does my help come from there?
> My help comes from the Lord,
>   who made heaven and earth!
>
> He will not let you stumble;
>   the one who watches over you will not slumber.
> Indeed, he who watches over Israel
>   never slumbers or sleeps.
>
> The Lord himself watches over you!
>   The Lord stands beside you as your protective shade.
> The sun will not harm you by day,
>   nor the moon at night.

> The LORD keeps you from all harm
> and watches over your life.
> The LORD keeps watch over you as you come and go,
> both now and forever.

LINGER

Read the passage again out loud. Are the same words or phrases you marked the first time still standing out? Write them down. How do these words or phrases apply to your life right now?

LEARN

As you read the text for the third time, ask yourself, How is God inviting me to respond? What does He want me to be learning from this? What am I noticing? Write out what comes to mind.

LIVE

Read the passage one last time and answer these questions:

Why is God showing me this now?

What does this mean for my life?

How do I need to live differently?

How do I need to respond to God's invitation?

Lord Jesus, help me to lift my eyes to You. To fix my gaze on You, Jesus. To set my mind and heart on things above. Give me the courage to cry out for help and to seek You when I face the battles ahead. You and You alone are where my help comes from. Thank You for that truth. Help me to believe it and live what I know is true. Amen.

My Prayer:

Where do you need help? What situations or circumstances do you need to lift to Jesus? How do you feel knowing God watches over you and never sleeps or slumbers—knowing there is nothing He doesn't see or know about? What do you need to hand over to Him to care for?

WEEK FOUR: REFLECT AND ACT

We've encountered an amazing story this week. A story of God's provision, no doubt, but also a story of how God's people fixed their eyes on Him as their rescue. Jehoshaphat led the people of Judah back to God, with all eyes on Him. They prayed. They worshiped. They did what mattered. Most of all, they were courageous, believing God for their deliverance. They did all that in the face of fear, trusting God for whatever would come—even calamity and possibly death. They surrendered to the will of the Father, worshiping Him at every turn.

Can the same be said of us? Remember that if war hasn't already knocked on your door, it's coming in some shape or form. We have an enemy who pursues us. What will our response be in the midst of the battle? Will we seek God? Will we surrender to God? Will we worship before we see the results? Will we continue to worship regardless of the outcome?

My prayer for you as you wrap up this week is that God will remind you of His great power in the midst of insurmountable odds. He is King of the world, after all. Take some time to sit with Him and review what you've learned this week. Ask Him to show up and show Himself. He loves to do that!

Take some time to answer each of these questions in your journal or in the space below:

What truths did God reveal through my time in His Word this week?

What challenged me?

What am I still struggling to believe?

What are God's invitations to me right now?

Are there themes or patterns in what God is showing me? If so, what are they?

What action steps do I need to follow as a result of what I've learned this week?

Let's trust the One who rescues, who provides, and who protects. The One who brings the victory. May you find rest on every side, but until you do, may your help come from the Lord, the Maker of heaven and earth.

God, may I see Your presence in this Your day, every day and every way.

All that I am, Lord, I place into Your hands.

The troubles that weary me, I place into Your hands.

The thoughts that disturb me, I place into Your hands.

I place into Your hands, Lord, the choices that I face.

Guard me from choosing the way perilous of which the end is heart-pain and the secret tear.

Rich in counsel, show us the way that is plain and safe.

May I feel Your presence at the heart of my desire, and so know it for Your desire for me. . . .

Help me to find my happiness in my acceptance of what is Your purpose for me:

> In friendly eyes, in work well done,
>
> In quietness born of trust,
>
> And, most of all, in the awareness of Your presence in my spirit.[27]

— OSWALD OF NORTHUMBRIA (605–642)

27. From Kurt Bjorklund, *Prayers for Today: A Yearlong Journey of Devotional Prayer* (Chicago: Moody. 2011), 42.

regardless, you are good

"Be still, and know that I am God;
I will be exalted among the nations, I will be exalted in the earth."
The Lord Almighty is with us; the God of Jacob is our fortress.

PSALM 46:10–11

We've been journeying together for four weeks now. We've covered a lot of ground and learned some new ways of thinking. I pray that as we enter into these final two weeks together, you find new mercies every morning and see God's faithfulness at every turn.

Last week we saw the remarkable hand of God at work as He showed up and protected His people from the calamity they feared. But that's not always the case. Certainly, God shows up in every circumstance, but we don't always dodge the casualties.

How do we respond, when our unknown becomes the known we feared?

This is the week where your time with God will matter most. Don't think of your study as "homework." These are times when you can receive a word from the Holy Spirit that no one else can give you. God knows your *whole story*—every single broken piece of it. Because of that, as you'll discover, He's able to care for you like no one else can. He's been in every moment with you—in the hard places and in the celebrations.

I pray this week you will begin to see how God showed up in the very places of your despair in spite of the fact you didn't see Him there in the beginning. But He's been there all along. And He's had a plan to redeem it all for His glory and His renown.

My prayer for us this week:

Lord Jesus, our lives have been hard, but You have been there all along. You have seen every moment and You hold every shattered piece of our stories. Help us trust You as we allow You to mend our hearts. Grow our confidence in You as we step into our unknown futures, knowing the brokenness of our pasts. Help us to believe You are still good. Amen.

INTRODUCTION TO WEEK 5

REGARDLESS, YOU ARE GOOD

Happy endings. We love them. The story we studied last week in 2 Chronicles 20 would make a great movie. The tension of war, desperation for a rescue, and ultimate victory are ingredients for an outcome we all love: a solid, feel-good finale.

But that's not always been my experience. My storyline isn't filled with happy endings. There have been times when I've even diligently done the very things Jehoshaphat and the people of Judah did to seek God and my circumstances didn't turn out well. Sometimes the feel-good finale eludes us.

What happens when there isn't a rosy outcome or when what we feared in the unknown becomes our reality?

How do we open our hands in surrender and say to God, "Okay. Whatever You say, I accept"? What does it take for us to say, "God, whatever You have for me—regardless of what may come, I will *choose* to believe You are good"?

This week may be a little tricky. I don't know your story, but I know you've experienced loss and grief along the way. More than likely, life hasn't turned out the way you anticipated it would. I don't know that I've ever met a person whose life has turned out *exactly* as planned. Regrets and losses have marked the stories of each of us.

What we do with these marker moments affects the way we move into the unknown. When we've endured calamity or trauma, it affects the way we view the future. We have a greater desire to be in control of our circumstances because we don't want to experience hurt again. Sometimes we even want to rewrite our stories so they don't have the dark spots at all.

At times, we want to paint a picture, cropping out the things we'd rather not see—those parts that are a little more difficult.[28]

---

28. If you have experienced a traumatic event in your life that has significantly marked your story, there is hope for healing. Wonderful, trained Christian counselors, spiritual directors, and pastors are available to walk with you in the healing process. Please contact your local church to find appropriate resources to take the first steps, or you can begin by visiting http://www.aacc.net/resources/find-a-counselor/ and looking for a licensed professional in your area.

This week we're going to look at another of my favorites, Psalm 46. I'm sure you are familiar with at least one phrase from this psalm: "Be still, and know that I am God" (v. 10). Perhaps you've seen a painting or plaque depicting these words as a restful scene you want to jump into and escape your chaotic life. But all the while you're thinking (at least I am) that this isn't what my *actual* life looks like.

This phrase is calming, but it's not the whole picture. I believe just pulling out these familiar words is a bit misleading. Let's read through all of Psalm 46 so we can zoom out and get a more complete view of what God is saying to us.

> God is our refuge and strength,
>   an ever-present help in trouble.
> Therefore we will not fear, though the earth give way
>   and the mountains fall into the heart of the sea,
> though its waters roar and foam
>   and the mountains quake with their surging.
>
> There is a river whose streams make glad the city of God,
>   the holy place where the Most High dwells.
> God is within her, she will not fall;
>   God will help her at break of day.
> Nations are in uproar, kingdoms fall;
>   he lifts his voice, the earth melts.
>
> The Lord Almighty is with us;
>   the God of Jacob is our fortress.
>
> Come and see what the Lord has done,
>   the desolations he has brought on the earth.
> He makes wars cease
>   to the ends of the earth.
> He breaks the bow and shatters the spear;
>   he burns the shields with fire.
> He says, "Be still, and know that I am God;

> I will be exalted among the nations,
> I will be exalted in the earth."
> The LORD Almighty is with us;
> the God of Jacob is our fortress.

What do we see when we zoom out? Chaos. Creation in turmoil. The waters rage, roar, and foam. The mountains quake and surge. Nations are in uproar. Kingdoms fall. The psalmist isn't just depicting a simple life tragedy, but describing the very order of creation falling apart.

Yet in this disordered confusion, we are reminded of some great truths about who God is. He is a refuge and strength. He is a safe place to hide. He provides shelter when the mountains crash all around. Even in the middle of the mess, God's protection covers us. He is an ever-present help, which in Hebrew means "a help that can be easily found when trouble comes."[29] The chaos doesn't change who God is. He is immovable. Unshakable. And He can be found when we need Him.

Is it possible we will be harmed by the raging waters or the falling earth? Sure, but the most important truth is found in the refrain of the psalm in verses 7 and 11. *"The LORD Almighty is with us; the God of Jacob is our fortress."* Our God isn't a far-off, unreachable God. He is Emmanuel, God *with* us. When we experience tragedy, God is right in the muck and the mire with us. He will never leave us or forsake us (Deut. 31:6). Peace can be the state of our souls when we realize God is *with* us in our pain and chaos.

The psalmist also refers to God as our fortress. This word in the Hebrew is *misgab*, meaning "a high place, a retreat, a secure height, a defense, a high fort, a refuge."[30] This type of fortress would have mirrored the ancient understanding of a city wall, the first line of defense for a town. It kept people safe inside and kept danger outside. God is our protector, just like the walls of an ancient city. He is the barrier, the deliverer, the One who keeps us safe.

When I say *safe*, I don't mean perfect or that God grants us a life of prosperity without harm. Remember, in the psalm, the world is crashing down. But even

---

29. Gerald H. Wilson, *Psalms*, vol. 1, *The NIV Application Commentary* (Grand Rapids, MI: Zondervan, 2002), 715–16.
30. *Misgab*. Blueletterbible.com. https://www.blueletterbible.org/lang/Lexicon/Lexicon.cfm?strongs=H4869&t=NASB.

so, He is the Keeper of our souls. He is the One who holds our hearts. He brings peace and guards us (Phil. 4:7).

What do we know just from this psalm about the nature of this God who is *with* us and serves as our fortress? Let's look at a few of the actions of God in this passage. Just read the list below and see the powerful characteristics of God displayed:

- He lifts his voice, the earth melts.
- He makes wars cease to the ends of the earth.
- He breaks the bow.
- He shatters the spear.
- He has brought desolations on the earth.
- He dwells in the holy place.
- He is within the holy place and will help her.
- He is with us.
- He is our fortress.
- He is our refuge and strength.
- He will be exalted among the nations and in the earth.
- He is God.

That is a pretty impressive list right there. This psalm speaks of radical trust in the face of overwhelming threat.[31] When we must choose radical trust, we must know in whom it is we are placing our trust. *This* is the God we can trust. He is powerful and unstoppable. He controls the universe (Col. 1:15–17) and He protects us at the same time.

If all of these things are true, then it is possible for us to live out Psalm 46:10, is it not? The phrase "be still" in the NASB says, "Cease striving." The Hebrew term for this means to cease and desist, much like a parent separating two fighting children. It doesn't really mean to be quiet or calm. It's more accurately understood as "stop what you have been doing and be still."[32]

31. Wilson, *Psalms*, 714.
32. Wilson, *Psalms*, 721.

If we're frantically struggling to hold our chaotic world together so we can avoid impending calamity or determine a specific outcome, how in the world will we ever experience God acting on our behalf? So, we are to be still. Cease striving. Quit trying so hard. Let go of the outcome and allow God to hold it for us.

It's much easier to do so when we know to whom we're handing the reins. Psalm 46 describes who God is. He's intense. He's powerful. The entire earth is going to bow down to Him. He can lift His voice and melt the earth. Even when everything is completely falling apart, where He dwells, there is peace. Where He lives, holy peace and joy can be found. Even in the midst of the chaos.

Psalm 46 shows us, yet again, the importance of looking at God and not at our circumstances—fixing our eyes on Jesus. We see the rich truths of the power of God in this text.

When we focus on *who* God is, knowing He is *with* us in the struggles we face, we see our circumstances and our stories very differently. Verse 10 doesn't say "cease striving because I've given you everything you need right now." It says "cease striving and *know* [experiential knowledge] that I am God."

> I am the One who is sovereign.
> I am the One who is in control.
> I am the One who holds the power.
> I am the One who will be exalted.

Nothing happens to you or me that has not first passed through the hand of God. The story of Job is a great illustration of God's firsthand knowledge of our tragedies. It also reveals the author of our pain—our very real enemy, Satan. Job endures calamity after calamity all at the hand of Satan, but with God's consent.[33] Satan was the author of Job's pain, but God was present with him in it.

What we must truly understand is that we live in a broken Eden. God designed the world to be perfect, without sin—beautiful like the garden of Eden was. When

---

33. We aren't going to be in the book of Job this week, but if you don't know the story of Job, it is well worth the read.

sin entered the picture, a lot was broken (Gen. 3). Here we are, thousands of years later, living in disease and broken relationships as a result. We're living in this skin that is as redeemed as it possibly can be at this time. Our world is broken. It just is until Christ returns and restores it all, which He has promised to do (Acts 1:11).

But even with the world in this state, God determined that Jesus would come and walk in our broken Eden in the same skin we wear, becoming familiar with our struggles. We have a High Priest who understands our weaknesses (Heb. 4:15), knowing what it means to be tempted (Matt. 4:1–11). We cry out to someone who grieved when His friend Lazarus died (John 11). He experienced physical pain when He was flogged, beaten, and then crucified (John 19). He knows what it means to experience the shaming words of others. He understands what it means to be falsely accused, to be mocked (John 19:11–16, 19).

He was a Man of Sorrows—acquainted with grief (Isa. 53:3), familiar with the hard things we encounter. When those things pass through His hands, I believe there is always a plan in His mind already for their redemption, for how it will be used for His glory. He knows how these hard things will grow us, shape us, change us, heal us. He sees that picture from the beginning. He still grieves with us, but He sits in a different seat than we do. He sees it all from beginning to end.

Becoming parents was a difficult road for Matt and me. When I began working in full-time ministry after nine years of teaching choral music, we were diagnosed with unexplainable infertility. There's nothing quite like an unexplained diagnosis. When a doctor looks at you and says, "Well, I can't tell you why," you have a tendency to ask God to answer the question for you. Here's an excerpt from my journal at the time:

> *There is so much going on with us right now, God. It's really kind of difficult to understand. I know You are in control and You have our lives in Your hands. I am afraid of what we are going to have to deal with. What are You preparing us for? Where are You taking us? Will we have to adopt all our children? Will I ever be able to experience a pregnancy and delivery and motherhood at its fullest?*

There are so many unanswered questions. Jesus, how did You face the cross with-out fear? I am fearful and what I am facing is so very little compared to what You endured . . . Sometimes I cannot understand Your love, God. The way You work and the ways You choose to change and shape us. I guess that is why You are God and I am not. God, I am trusting You—help me to trust You fully. It's so difficult when everything seems so up in the air![34]

When we stand on the edge of the unknown facing the great possibility of pain, trusting God is difficult. All I wanted to do was minimize my hurt. I hoped God would spare us from being broken any more.

As we waited for answers, we were approached by a well-meaning woman from our church who connected us to someone facilitating Russian adoptions. This introduction seemed like an answer to our prayers to become parents. We were thrilled! We wanted a baby and we were told there were Russian women looking for American parents for their children. It seemed like a win-win to us.

I couldn't believe God was answering our prayers so quickly.

We are still waiting on information about our possible Russian baby. We are praying for a girl—Hannah Mikhaila. I am sure she is beautiful. . . . Sometimes it is difficult to even fathom, but I know You, Lord, are capable of orchestrating something of this magnitude. You are so amazing! I can't even believe it most of the time, but I know You are able. I pray you will prepare Matt and me for whatever it is you have in store for us. Having a beautiful daughter would be such a gift![35]

God was preparing us for what was in store, but it certainly wasn't what we thought. After actively pursuing this adoption, we woke to a knock on our door. On the other side of the door were two FBI agents. One was a victim's specialist and the other an investigating agent on our case. After a month of praying over a photograph of a baby girl we'd named Hannah, we discovered the adoption opportunity was a scam. There were no babies.

34. Personal journal entry, July 9, 2005.
35. Personal journal entry, August 12, 2005.

My heart shattered as we sat at the kitchen table listening to the agent repeat over and over again there was no evidence of any babies. How could this happen? How could we follow God and pray and have *this* be the outcome? We had a room filled with clothes and a crib and there wasn't even a baby to grieve.

But God was ever-present. As I wept for weeks and stared at the ceiling fan in our bedroom, He was *with* me. He was with me in ways I'd never known. It hurt so much, *but He was there*. His peace and comfort were real. He was there when I had to redo my makeup in the church parking lot before going into work because I had cried it all off on the way to the office. He was there when I had to stand on the stage and lead worship in front of our congregation, singing Matt Redman's lyric, "Blessed be Your name when I'm found in the desert place." He was there. And I *knew* it.

Over the next few months, God opened another chance to adopt a child. I don't think I need to explain how terrified we were. Talk about what ifs! Would this happen again? If it did, would we be able to survive it? We had absolutely no idea what the answers were to any of those questions, but God was leading, so we followed.

Almost one year after our initial diagnosis, our daughter, Abigail, was placed in our arms. In that moment, God stitched our hearts up a bit more. Through the pain, it was so hard to see all the ways He broke open our hearts so there would be more room for her. But He did.

I cannot begin to tell you the countless places where we saw God's fingerprints in our story. Looking back, I can see them all over every little detail. He was orchestrating our story like a masterful game of chess. We have the choice to focus on the pain or on the fingerprints of God. In the moment, it's sometimes impossible to see them, but as we reflect and look back, they are clearly evident.

Grief is not something the American culture does very well. First of all, our culture only really grieves when someone dies. We didn't bury anyone in our story, so it was hard for us to grieve. But we still lost *a lot*. Loss is a part of life, so we each experience losses all the time. We lose jobs, dreams die, friendships end, marriages sometimes shatter. We lose something we thought we were going to have.

When I traveled to Israel, I was struck by the grieving process in this culture, when the community we visited had experienced a sudden death of a loved one. In Israel, they spend an entire week grieving. They drink a special coffee, more bitter than their usual coffee—which is pretty bitter to begin with! They wear no color. There is no laughter or dancing or joyous music. They open their homes for the entire week and people come and just sit in their living room with them. Sometimes they sit in silence (as Job's friends did in Job 2:13). Sometimes they weep and wail. They simply allow their grief to be what it is—heart-wrenching hurt. But *you sit with them.* They share it with you. And you allow them to feel it. You are present in their trouble.

Just like Emmanuel—*God with us.*

We have to grieve our losses. When we don't grieve, allowing God and others to be present with us in our pain, we carry the grief forward with us. It settles in our souls in a different way. It affects our view of God when we don't allow Him to heal us. Instead, we should begin to ask ourselves, "Where has God shown up in my losses? How has He cared for me in the middle of my grief?" These questions help us notice God's hand at work in our darkest seasons and changes the way we view those events and circumstances.

I love the words Habakkuk writes in chapter 3:

> Though the fig tree does not bud
>   and there are no grapes on the vines,
> though the olive crop fails
>   and the fields produce no food,
> though there are no sheep in the pen
>   and no cattle in the stalls,
> yet I will rejoice in the LORD,
>   I will be joyful in God my Savior.

We think joy is an outward expression, requiring jazz hands, a big smile, and a splash of sparkles. Joy is more, it's a fruit of the Spirit (Gal. 5:22). It's something that dwells within us because of the Spirit's work. It is an inner state of being. It's not an outward expression nor is it based on external circumstances. At times our hearts will overflow into our expressions, but it starts with what's inside. The big question we have to ask ourselves is this: can I rejoice in the Lord even when difficult things are happening to me?

James puts it this way:

> Consider it pure joy, my brothers and sisters, whenever you face trials of many kinds, because you know that the testing of your faith produces perseverance. Let perseverance finish its work so that you may be mature and complete, not lacking anything. (James 1:2–4)

Consider it pure joy? *Really?* Why? Because these moments are our teachers. They are the spaces where we learn about the relentless pursuit of our amazing God. They provide a training ground that tests our faith and grows it. Through persevering in the difficulties, we become mature and complete, not lacking anything.

Looking back at this hard season in my life, I find a long list of things I would have never learned in any other way. I discovered who God truly was. I saw characteristics of God in action that moved me from a *gnosis* knowledge to *epignosis* knowledge. There were places where I tasted and saw that God was indeed good. I learned a great deal about God as we waited for Him to move on our behalf.

It was too hard. It was just too much. But when we do look back, we can see God's hand at work. We can see the simple places He orchestrated things for our good. We're reminded of His presence in our pain.

We all go through times of waiting.[36] We all experience loss. We all have to grieve. Our losses are an important part of the story God is writing within us. Often we don't want to look back on hard times because we just want to forget. It was too painful. But when we do look back, we can see God's hand at work.

Through it all, He is here. He always has been. *God with us.*

LISTEN AND LINGER

Take a moment to read through Psalm 46.

When have you experienced God's presence with you in your pain?

How have you seen His hand as you reflect back on your greatest losses?

---

36. While we were waiting for our baby, someone shared the poem "Wait" © 2003 by Russell Kelfer with us. You can find this beautiful work at www.dtm.org.

What have you learned about God's goodness through your setbacks and in the hard places?

When have you had to wait on God? What did you learn about Him in the waiting?

WEEK 5 | DAY 1

GOD WITH US

Remember that tranquil scene you can imagine illustrating Psalm 46:10? "Be still, and know that I am God." This phrase certainly depicts the peace of God, but doesn't show the depth of the passage where the verse is nestled. The greater picture has been cropped.

Looking at the big picture, we see that chaos is the scene. The need to cling to something greater, stronger, bigger runs through the entire psalm. The psalmist also shows the sovereign, mighty power of God who holds the universe together as it collapses. God is a fortress, a great shield around His people.

At times, I have felt as though my entire world is crashing around me. I'm finding more and more what it means to be peacefully sitting somewhere quiet while the waves crash outside the fortress God's provided. I've spent my fair share of time striving and trying to control the speed at which the mountains fall. In the end, I just end up exhausted and a bit scraped up. Allow these words to wash over you today as you read them. Ask God to show you where you need to allow Him to be God.

Before you begin to read today, take a look at the following words and their Hebrew definitions:

- Present—*matsa*: to find, secure; to meet, encounter; to be found to be discovered; to appear, be recognized.[37]

- Stronghold—*misgab*: a high place, refuge, secure height, retreat.[38]

- Cease—*raphah*: to sink, relax, sink down, let drop; withdraw; to let go; to show oneself slack.[39]

- Know—*yada*: to know; to perceive; to know by experience; to recognize, admit, acknowledge, confess; to consider; to be acquainted with.[40]

37. Blueletterbible.org, *Matsa*.
38. Blueletterbible.org, *Misgab*.
39. Blueletterbible.org, *Raphah*.
40. Blueletterbible.org, *Yada*.

With these word definitions in mind, read through Psalm 46 in the New American Standard Bible, printed below. Sit quietly for a moment before you begin. Ask the Holy Spirit to speak and show you what the Lord wants for you in this passage. Mark words or phrases that stand out as you read.

God is our refuge and strength,
A very present help in trouble.
Therefore we will not fear, though the earth should change
And though the mountains slip into the heart of the sea;
Though its waters roar and foam,
Though the mountains quake at its swelling pride. . . .

There is a river whose streams make glad the city of God,
The holy dwelling places of the Most High.
God is in the midst of her, she will not be moved;
God will help her when morning dawns.
The nations made an uproar, the kingdoms tottered;
He raised His voice, the earth melted.
The Lord of hosts is with us;
The God of Jacob is our stronghold. . . .

Come, behold the works of the Lord,
Who has wrought desolations in the earth.
He makes wars to cease to the end of the earth;
He breaks the bow and cuts the spear in two;
He burns the chariots with fire.
"Cease striving and know that I am God;
I will be exalted among the nations, I will be exalted in the earth."
The Lord of hosts is with us;
The God of Jacob is our stronghold. . . .

Read the passage again out loud. This time read it in the New Living Translation. What words or phrases stand out in this translation? Write them down. Are they similar to what you marked in the previous version? How do these words or phrases apply to your life right now?

God is our refuge and strength,
    always ready to help in times of trouble.
So we will not fear when earthquakes come
    and the mountains crumble into the sea.
Let the oceans roar and foam.
    Let the mountains tremble as the waters surge! . . .

A river brings joy to the city of our God,
    the sacred home of the Most High.
God dwells in that city; it cannot be destroyed.
    From the very break of day, God will protect it.
The nations are in chaos,
    and their kingdoms crumble!
God's voice thunders,
    and the earth melts!
The Lord of Heaven's Armies is here among us;
    the God of Israel is our fortress. . . .

Come, see the glorious works of the Lord:
    See how he brings destruction upon the world.
He causes wars to end throughout the earth.
    He breaks the bow and snaps the spear;
    he burns the shields with fire.

"Be still, and know that I am God!
    I will be honored by every nation.
    I will be honored throughout the world."

The LORD of Heaven's Armies is here among us;
the God of Israel is our fortress. . . .

LEARN

As you read the text for the third time in The Message, write out any distinct phrases from this version that stand out. Are they similar to the previous versions? Ask yourself, "How is God inviting me to respond? What does He want me to be learning from this? What am I noticing?" Write out what comes to mind.

God is a safe place to hide,
ready to help when we need him.
We stand fearless at the cliff-edge of doom,
courageous in seastorm and earthquake,
Before the rush and roar of oceans,
the tremors that shift mountains.

Jacob-wrestling God fights for us,
GOD-of-Angel-Armies protects us.

River fountains splash joy, cooling God's city,
this sacred haunt of the Most High.
God lives here, the streets are safe,
God at your service from crack of dawn.
Godless nations rant and rave, kings and kingdoms threaten,
but Earth does anything he says.

Jacob-wrestling God fights for us,
    God-of-Angel-Armies protects us.

Attention, all! See the marvels of God!
    He plants flowers and trees all over the earth,
Bans war from pole to pole,
    breaks all the weapons across his knee.
"Step out of the traffic! Take a long,
    loving look at me, your High God,
    above politics, above everything."

Jacob-wrestling God fights for us,
    God-of-Angel-Armies protects us.

LIVE

Read the passage one last time in the New International Version. Mark words or phrases that jump off the page in this translation. Look back at your previous readings. What do you notice? Do you see themes? Take a moment to answer these questions:

Why is God showing me this now?

What does this mean for my life?

How do I need to live differently?

How do I need to respond to God's invitation?

God is our refuge and strength,
    an ever-present help in trouble.
Therefore we will not fear, though the earth give way
    and the mountains fall into the heart of the sea,
though its waters roar and foam
    and the mountains quake with their surging.

There is a river whose streams make glad the city of God,
    the holy place where the Most High dwells.
God is within her, she will not fall;
    God will help her at break of day.
Nations are in uproar, kingdoms fall;
    he lifts his voice, the earth melts.

The Lord Almighty is with us;
    the God of Jacob is our fortress.

Come and see what the Lord has done,
    the desolations he has brought on the earth.
He makes wars cease
    to the ends of the earth.
He breaks the bow and shatters the spear;
    he burns the shields with fire.
He says, "Be still, and know that I am God;
    I will be exalted among the nations,
    I will be exalted in the earth."

The Lord Almighty is with us;
   the God of Jacob is our fortress.

Almighty God, You are my refuge, my hiding place. My strong tower in the middle of the intense battle. Protect me, Father. Keep me from buckling under the pressure of my circumstances. Give me Your strength. You are my Deliverer. Thank You for that truth. Help me to believe it and live what I know is true. Amen.

My Prayer:

Journaling Prompt:

Where in your life have you seen God be a refuge and strength for you? How do you feel knowing God is with you in the midst of even the most difficult circumstances? How does Psalm 46:10 change for you as you look at the actual context of the verse? Where do you need God to be an ever-present help for you right now?

COME WHAT MAY

Growing up in the church, we spent a lot of time at the church building. If the church was open, we were there. Sunday mornings, Sunday evenings, Wednesday evenings, and at times one other night for either a rehearsal of some kind or another Bible study. I have always enjoyed being with God's people. Sometimes, though, going to church can be hard. Walking into the building with a smile plastered on your face when your life just shattered is, at times, the last thing you want to do.

There have been times in my life when worship seemed impossible. I could barely sing without a full-on meltdown including a snotty ugly cry. As a worship leader, that seems like a ridiculous thing to say, but it's absolutely true. There have been seasons of excruciating waiting. Spaces where dreams died. Months and months of grieving over loss. Times when relationships struggled.

We are told we *will* have trouble (John 16:33a). If you haven't experienced any trouble in your life, I hate to be the one to tell you, but it's probably coming. Here's what we know: We are not to fear when the earth gives way (Ps. 46:2). When trouble comes, we are to take heart and remember that Jesus has overcome the world (John 16:33b). We have a God who is an ever-present help in that trouble (Ps. 46:1). Our God has equipped us with what we need for whatever season lies ahead.

And He is *with* us.

He is a fortress. A refuge and strength. He is a shield about us. Our Protector. Our Rescuer.

God doesn't change when our circumstances do (James 1:17). He is faithful and good even when calamity comes. That means He is always worthy of our worship.

Remember, worship matters. We saw how pivotal worship is in the story of Jehoshaphat. It changes us, not our circumstances. It changes the way we view our situation. It changes our hearts.

When I think of the stories of Esther and of Shadrach, Meshach, and Abednego, I'm stunned by their resolve. In the midst of when the Jews, including Queen Esther, faced impending death, she chose to rely on God for courage and strength and decided she would go before the king on behalf of her people—though doing so without an invitation was a capital offense and she could be executed. But "if I perish, I perish," she said (Est. 4:16). She obeyed God regardless of what the unknown outcome might be, without knowing how God would show up.

Shadrach, Meshach, and Abednego refused to bow down to worship the huge golden idol King Nebuchadnezzar had ordered to be erected. They chose to worship God and God alone. They stood their ground as they stared into the unknown of their punishment, being thrown into the blazing hot fiery furnace. They believed God could save them, but they didn't know if He would. They told the king, "But even if he does not, we want you to know, Your Majesty, that we will not serve your gods or worship the image of gold you have set up" (Dan. 3:18).

Even if.

Even if God doesn't do what we hope He will do, we will still praise Him.

Even if God chooses something other than what we're praying for, we will worship and bow down to Him.

Come what may.

When we can say, "*Yet*, I will still praise you," we are transformed. Our circumstances may be exactly the same, but *we're different* as a result of our sacrifice of praise. At times, it is truly a sacrifice to praise in challenging seasons.

Today we are going to examine two passages of Scripture, from Habakkuk and Lamentations. Take some time to allow these passages to soak into your soul. Give yourself some space to remember moments when worship has been harder for you—those seasons when praising was truly a sacrifice. Maybe you're in one of those seasons right now. Ask God to hold your heart as you allow His words to wash over you. May healing come as a result and may we all be able to say with confidence, "Yet, I will still praise you, O God."

LISTEN

Read through the excerpts from Habakkuk and Lamentations below. Sit quietly for a moment before you begin. Ask the Holy Spirit to speak and show you what the Lord wants for you in this passage. Mark words or phrases that stand out as you read.

> I trembled inside when I heard this;
>   my lips quivered with fear.
> My legs gave way beneath me,
>   and I shook in terror.
> I will wait quietly for the coming day
>   when disaster will strike the people who invade us.
> Even though the fig trees have no blossoms,
>   and there are no grapes on the vines;
> even though the olive crop fails,
>   and the fields lie empty and barren;
> even though the flocks die in the fields,
>   and the cattle barns are empty,
> yet I will rejoice in the LORD!
>   I will be joyful in the God of my salvation!
> The Sovereign LORD is my strength!
>   He makes me as surefooted as a deer,
>   able to tread upon the heights.
> (Hab. 3:16–19 NLT)

I have been deprived of peace;
    I have forgotten what prosperity is.
So I say, "My splendor is gone
    and all that I had hoped from the Lord."

I remember my affliction and my wandering,
    the bitterness and the gall.
I well remember them,
    and my soul is downcast within me.
Yet this I call to mind
    and therefore I have hope:

Because of the Lord's great love we are not consumed,
    for his compassions never fail.
They are new every morning;
    great is your faithfulness.
I say to myself, "The Lord is my portion;
    therefore I will wait for him."

The Lord is good to those whose hope is in him,
    to the one who seeks him;
it is good to wait quietly
    for the salvation of the Lord.
(Lam. 3:17–26)

LINGER

Read the passages again out loud. Are the same words or phrases you marked the first time still standing out? Write them down. How do these words or phrases apply to your life right now?

LEARN

As you read the text for the third time, ask yourself, "How is God inviting me to respond? What does He want me to be learning from this? What am I noticing?" Write out what comes to mind.

LIVE

Read the passages one last time and answer these questions:

Why is God showing me this now?

What does this mean for my life?

How do I need to live differently?

How do I need to respond to God's invitation?

Lord Jesus, even in the midst of dark times, You are faithful. Even when the unthinkable happens, You are good. You hold me together. You bring me peace. Turn my eyes toward You in difficult times. Help me to worship You come what may. For You alone are worthy and You alone are unchangeable. Thank You for these truths. Help me to believe them and live what I know is true. Amen.

My Prayer:

Journaling Prompt:

When has it been difficult for you to worship God? What circumstances in your life have affected or are currently affecting your ability to worship God? Have you ever been able to worship God in really difficult circumstances? If so, what was that like? If not, how do you think worship would have changed your outlook? Where do you need to say, "Even if" right now?

WEEK 5 | DAY 3

TRIALS AND JOY, REALLY?

I love a good oxymoron. You know those? Phrases like jumbo shrimp or act naturally or artificial grass. The definition of an oxymoron is "a figure of speech by which a locution produces an incongruous, seemingly self-contradictory effect."[41] Fancy, right? Well, our texts today seem a little oxymoronic to me. Weakness brings strength? Consider trials joyous? Suffering produces character?

I know. These are *technically* not oxymorons, but they sure don't make much sense without a little effort. But I'm learning they are indeed true. When I look back over the course of my life, I see the many places where I've encountered trials—either of my own choosing or ones that chose me—and I'm markedly different as a result. Different in a good way.

These were times when God showed me a part of His character I would have never experienced otherwise. I've seen His faithfulness and strategy unfold in every hard place in my history. I wouldn't trade it for anything. Was I happy while it was happening? Absolutely not. But happiness isn't the same thing as joy. Joy is a fruit of the Spirit (Gal. 5:22). It's an internal spring that isn't affected by external conditions, as happiness is. It's not a feeling. It's a characteristic of God's nature within us. Because of this truth, it just might be possible to face trials and experience joy simultaneously.

Today we're encountering three different texts to glean a better understanding of what trials can produce within us. We can lean into this upside-down way of thinking that seems like an oxymoron, but it is actually just what living in the kingdom of God looks like. We're going to use the SOAP study method to dive into passages from Romans, 2 Corinthians, and James. Here we go!

---

41. Oxymoron. Dictionary.com. *Dictionary.com Unabridged.* http://www.dictionary.com/browse/oxymoron?s=t.

S for Scripture:

Read slowly through the Scriptures below. Mark the words or phrases as you go that have an impact on you.

Therefore, since we have been justified through faith, we have peace with God through our Lord Jesus Christ, through whom we have gained access by faith into this grace in which we now stand. And we boast in the hope of the glory of God. Not only so, but we also glory in our sufferings, because we know that suffering produces perseverance; perseverance, character; and character, hope. And hope does not put us to shame, because God's love has been poured out into our hearts through the Holy Spirit, who has been given to us.

You see, at just the right time, when we were still powerless, Christ died for the ungodly. Very rarely will anyone die for a righteous person, though for a good person someone might possibly dare to die. But God demonstrates his own love for us in this: While we were still sinners, Christ died for us. (Rom. 5:1–8)

Therefore, in order to keep me from becoming conceited, I was given a thorn in my flesh, a messenger of Satan, to torment me. Three times I pleaded with the Lord to take it away from me. But he said to me, "My grace is sufficient for you, for my power is made perfect in weakness." Therefore, I will boast all the more gladly about my weaknesses, so that Christ's power may rest on me. That is why, for Christ's sake, I delight in weaknesses, in insults, in hardships, in persecutions, in difficulties. For when I am weak, then I am strong. (2 Cor. 12:7–10)

Consider it pure joy, my brothers and sisters, whenever you face trials of many kinds, because you know that the testing of your faith produces perseverance. Let perseverance finish its work so that you may be mature and complete, not lacking anything. If any of you lacks wisdom, you should ask God, who gives generously to all without finding fault, and it will be given to you. But when you ask, you must believe and not doubt, because the one who doubts is like a wave of the sea, blown and tossed by the wind. That person should not expect to receive anything from the Lord. Such a person is double-minded and unstable in all they do.

Believers in humble circumstances ought to take pride in their high position. But the rich should take pride in their humiliation—since they will pass away like a wild flower. For the sun rises with scorching heat and withers the plant; its blossom falls and its beauty is destroyed. In the same way, the rich will fade away even while they go about their business.

Blessed is the one who perseveres under trial because, having stood the test, that person will receive the crown of life that the Lord has promised to those who love him.

When tempted, no one should say, "God is tempting me." For God cannot be tempted by evil, nor does he tempt anyone; but each person is tempted when they are dragged away by their own evil desire and enticed. Then, after desire has conceived, it gives birth to sin; and sin, when it is full-grown, gives birth to death.

Don't be deceived, my dear brothers and sisters. Every good and perfect gift is from above, coming down from the Father of the heavenly lights, who does not change like shifting shadows. (James 1:2–17)

O for Observation:

What are your observations about the text?

What do you notice?

What stands out?

What's going on in the texts?

What do you see that's repeated?

What are the main ideas?

Are there any important phrases they share?

What are the truths in these passages?

Take a moment to write down the benefits of trials.

What does each passage state trials or suffering will produce within us?

A for Application:
How is God calling you to apply the truth in this Scripture to your life right now? What is He calling you to change? How is He inviting you to be different?

Where have you seen these things to be true in your own life?

Where do you need to begin believing they will be true right now?

P for Prayer:

Heavenly Father, I want to choose joy even in the hard places. Teach me what trials actually produce in my life. Show me where I have learned these truths already. You are always at work to grow me into Your image, Jesus. Thank You for that truth. Help me to believe it and live what I know is true. Amen.

My Prayer:

What can you pray as a result of what God is calling you to do in this passage? What do you need to praise God for, confess to God, or request of Him in response?

Journaling Prompt:

How would choosing to see trials as joy change your perspective? How have you seen growth in your own life through trials and temptations? When have you seen God be strong in your weakness? When has perseverance made a difference in your life?

WEEK 5 DAY 4

CAST YOUR CARES

Remember my fiercely independent, pigtailed daughter, Abigail, declaring she could do it all by herself? Last week on Day 5, we discovered our help comes from the Lord, the Maker of heaven and earth. Even though we know this to be true, we still struggle with asking for the help we need. Our self-sufficient surroundings don't help us in this department.

We don't want to be a burden, and if you're like me, you feel like you should just be able to get it right on your own sometimes. It's even more difficult if you've been hurt before. That breach of trust spills into the places where we need help in the future. It can even affect the way we ask God for help.

What Scripture tells us, however, is to ask. A lot. We're told over and over God is our help, our refuge, a safe place to hide. He's our Sustainer. Our Redeemer. Our Protector. He's the source of our strength and deliverance.

So why don't we always seek Him in times of need? Why don't we trust Him when things don't go as planned?

Today we're taking a look at three passages that invite us to cast our cares on God. This word "cast" in the Hebrew is the word *shalak*. It means "to throw, hurl, fling, shed, throw away."[42] The Greek word is *epirrhipto* and has the same meaning as the Hebrew—"to throw upon."[43] It means we don't just place our cares on God, we hurl them at Him, which means *they are away from us*. We don't carry them anymore. The burden is no longer ours. With all the strength we can muster, we heave our cares on the massive, capable shoulders of the almighty God. He can handle it, I promise.

42. James Strong, *A Concise Dictionary of the Words in the Greek Testament and The Hebrew Bible* (Bellingham, WA: Logos Bible Software, 2009), 117.
43. James Strong, 31.

Before we begin reading today, write down some of your current cares and burdens that need to be hurled in the direction of Jesus.[44]

Look up 1 Peter 5:7 and Philippians 4:6–7 in your Bible. In the space below write both of these verses. Mark words or phrases that stand out. Get creative in how you write them out, if you want!

With these texts in mind, use the SOAP study method to study Psalm 55.

S for Scripture:

Read slowly through Psalm 55 in your own Bible. Mark words or phrases that stand out to you. Jot them down.

---

44. This practice is one I do often in my journaling. I put a box in the middle of the page and label it with the word associated with the things I'm listing. Then I create a "mind map" around the word, drawing lines to that word in the middle of the page. This allows me to see everything that is contributing to my burdens. I first saw this practice in *Write for Your Soul* by Jeff and Mindy Caliguire (Soul Care Communications, 1999). You can write the word "cares" in the middle of the page and draw everything around it that is contributing.

O for Observation:

What are your observations about the text? What do you notice? What stands out?

A for Application:

How is God calling you to apply the truth in this Scripture to your life right now? What is He calling you to change? How is He inviting you to be different?

P for Prayer:

PRAYER FOR THE DAY

Most High God, I long to trust You with all that I am. Teach me to cast my cares on You, Jesus. You will carry me when things are tough. Even in the hard seasons and in difficulty, You sustain me. Thank You for that truth. Help me to believe it and live what I know is true. Amen.

My Prayer:

What can you pray as a result of what God is calling you to do in this passage? What do you need to praise God for, confess to God, or request of Him in response?

Journaling Prompt:

When have you seen God show up in your circumstances and care for you? How has God sustained you in the past? What cares do you need to cast on Jesus in this season? What do you need to cry out to God for in this moment? How do you know you can trust Him?

WEEK 5 | DAY 5

THE PROMISE OF HEAVEN

Are you a dreamer? I'm not sure I know many dreamers these days. Maybe there are a few who dream, but I think we've been somewhat lulled to sleep by the world of Netflix and social media. We've forgotten the promises of a real place where our situations will no longer cause any pain.

I like to think of myself as a bit of a dreamer, but I don't typically spend much time dreaming about heaven. I think it's because it seems so far off—so unlike anything I've ever experienced here on this earth in this skin. I think when we don't dream (or even think) about it at all, we lose a little more hope.

You see, there *is* a day coming when all will be made new. A moment *will* come when we see Jesus face to face in the light of His full glory. Time will stand still and we'll no longer have to deal with the broken Eden or the sins of our flesh or the disappointment others bring or the loss of those we love or the death of dreams we once had when we were still actually dreaming.

As we wrap up this week's study, I want to remind you that heaven is a real place with real promises. God gave us a glimpse of it in Revelation. While the reality of the promise won't take away your pain or change your situation now, it *can* grow hope in you. And hope does not disappoint us (Rom. 5:5 NASB). Our hope dwells with God—in His presence and with His promises in mind.

Today, let's put ourselves in the scene. What will it be like to see this all become our reality? What will it feel like to be in the presence of Jesus? To live a life with no more tears or pain? Remembering the context we've already discovered this week, let's dig into the promises of what's to come in these passages from Revelation.

Read through Revelation 21:1–7 and 21:22–22:6 in your own Bible. Don't worry about historical or contextual accuracy. Just allow God to bring the story to life.

Allow Him to paint a picture for you—just as John, the author of Revelation, would have experienced it.

Write down some of the major things you are noticing.

What are your observations about the text?

What do you notice?

Now read through Revelation 21:1–7 and 21:22–22:6 in your own Bible again and begin to imagine the scene as if you were right in the middle of it.

What do you see?

What do you hear?

What do you smell?

Who is there?

What are you feeling?

What are you not feeling?

What's the mood of the place?

What do you think of it all?

What questions do you have?

What fears do you have?

What is God calling you to do as a result of this passage?

What are His invitations to you as you read through this text?

How do you need to live differently?

PRAYER FOR THE DAY

Lord Jesus, You are preparing this place for me. You are building a new Eden, a new Jerusalem where I won't experience the pain and suffering and the fear and anxiety that I experience here on earth. Remind me that Your promise of heaven is true. You are trustworthy. Help me to remember that this place Your Word describes is not a fantasy, but will be a reality one day. Thank You for that truth. Help me to believe it and what I know is true. Amen.

My Prayer:

Journaling Prompt:

How does knowing heaven is a sure promise help you in the here and now? How does the hope of this promise change your view of your current situation or past painful circumstances? What would it take for you to remember this hope for the future you have in Christ?

WEEK FIVE: REFLECT AND ACT

I'm not sure what your situation currently is or what it has been in the past. We all carry burdens and broken pieces of our stories. It's inevitable in a broken Eden. Calamity comes. Casualties happen. Sometimes we choose them and other times they choose us. All I know is, in the end, we can't avoid them.

But in the midst of it all, God is present. *He is here,* stewarding our stories and holding our hearts. He sustains us. He brings peace in the most tumultuous storms. He lavishes grace and love and mercy on us in our brokenness. That's something worth clinging to. That's something worth believing in. That's something worth surrendering to.

Take some time today to pore over this week's discoveries. Remember, we won't have lasting change if we don't take time for reflection. May God's grace and peace be palpable and His loving presence be tangible as you do.

Take some time to answer each of these questions in your journal:

What new truths did God reveal through my time in His Word this week?

What challenged me?

What am I still struggling to believe?

What are God's invitations to me right now?

Are there themes or patterns in what God is showing me? If so, what are they?

What action steps do I need to follow as a result of what I've learned this week?

Jesus is worth it. Every time.

And eventually the joy will come. The hope will rise. The healing will happen. I'm praying you will believe these truths and will live as though they are true.

I thank thee, O Lord, my Lord, for my being, my life . . .

For my redemption, my regeneration, my instruction in the Christian faith;

For thy forbearance and long suffering, thy prolonged forbearance, many a time, and many a year;

For all the benefits I have received, and all the undertakings wherein I have prospered;

For any good I may have done;
For the use of the blessings of this life;
For thy promise, and my hope of the enjoyment of good things to come;

For all these and also for all other mercies, known and unknown, . . .
I praise thee, I bless thee, I thank thee.[45]

—LANCELOT ANDREWES (1555–1626)

45. From Kurt Bjorklund, *Prayers for Today: A Yearlong Journey of Devotional Prayer* (Chicago: Moody, 2011), 191.

i will remember

I will remember the deeds of the LORD;
yes, I will remember your miracles of long ago.
I will consider all your works and meditate on all your mighty deeds.
PSALM 77:11–12

It's our final week together. I'm praying you are finding God in new, extraordinary ways. I'm praying you are choosing courage and strength as you face your unknowns head-on with God leading the way.

This week we will encounter the significance of remembering in our relationship with God and our experience with fear and anxiety. Remembering what God has done changes our view of *everything*.

We're going to look at a remarkable story in the Old Testament to gain a new perspective on remembering. We're going to recall our own memorial stones this week—the places in our lives that have been turning points, moments of transformation for us. Both wins and losses. These moments shape who we are in ways we don't always realize until we take a step back and name them, seeing God's presence in the midst of them.

I'm praying for you as you journey through your own history this week. Praying for courage. For eyes to see how God has shown up over and over again. Let's set our minds on things above as we remember what our Jesus has done for us.

My prayer for us this week:

Lord Jesus,
Oh, how we long for all that remembering brings to our lives! Help us to be a people who talk about what You have done for us. Help us to keep the works of Your hands crossing our lips. As they do, empower us with greater faith that propels us into the unseen path You've set before us. Help grow our trust in You as we remember what You've done throughout all of history.
Amen.

INTRODUCTION TO WEEK 6

I WILL REMEMBER

The human memory is a remarkable mystery.

An unexpected taste transports us to that recipe served at every holiday gathering. A whiff of a specific perfume reminds us of a dear loved one. A few notes of a certain song carry us back to our first junior high breakup (that maybe we'd like to forget). It's amazing to know how much our memories can hold and that simple triggers can bring those memories to the surface.

At the same time, I'm astounded by how quickly we can forget. We get busy and distracted. God knows we are a forgetful people. He knew we would need to be reminded of the things that matter most. Over and over again, God reminds His people to remember.

We tend to forget what we don't remember. Profound, I know. Maybe it's completely obvious, but what we don't purposefully remember gets lost—forgotten. God knew what happens in us when we forget.

> When the LORD your God brings you into the land he swore to your fathers, to Abraham, Isaac and Jacob, to give you—a land with large, flourishing cities you did not build, houses filled with all kinds of good things you did not provide, wells you did not dig, and vineyards and olive groves you did not plant—then when you eat and are satisfied, **be careful that you do not forget the LORD**, **who brought you out of Egypt, out of the land of slavery.** (Deut. 6:10–12)

The Hebrew word for "forget" used in this passage is *sakah*. It means "to forget, ignore, overlook, be unmindful, *not remember information or to lose sight of its significance*.[46] When we are unmindful, we forget and lose sight of the significance of what God has done. We overlook His provision in our lives and begin to give ourselves credit for things we simply did not do.

---

46. James Swanson, *Dictionary of Biblical Languages with Semantic Domains: Hebrew (Old Testament)*, electronic ed., DBLH 8894. Oak Harbor, WA: Logos Research Systems, Inc., 1997.

When life is rolling along and our needs are met, it can be easy to slip into the mindset that we built what is around us. We begin to believe our hands put it all together. We think that our cleverness or skills or positions, whatever they are, earned us our families, our homes, and everything within. When we think we built it, we tend to think it's our responsibility to hold it all together too.

In Joshua 3 and 4, the Israelites witness another of God's mind-blowing miracles. He gives them some specific instructions to ensure they will remember the moment. The scene is phenomenal. The Israelites are so close to entering the Promised Land, they can practically taste the milk and honey.

The first obstacle on their journey is the Jordan River. When they reach it, it is at flood stage—not optimal river-crossing conditions. The people are following the ark. Where the ark goes, they go. This is not Noah's ark, so they won't be cruising across the flood-stage river. This is the ark of the covenant, which protected sacred objects and also symbolized God's presence with His people.

God gave Joshua instructions. Joshua explained to Israel what the Lord was going to do. "As soon as the priests who carry the ark of the Lord—the Lord of all the earth—set foot in the Jordan, its waters flowing downstream will be cut off and stand up in a heap" (Josh. 3:13). They'd heard the stories of how God saved their ancestors from the Egyptians—how their enemies drowned in the Red Sea. They'd sung songs about it. They'd sat around every Sabbath meal and every Passover meal as they heard it recounted over and over again. Because God parted the waters before, they knew He could do it again.

And He did.

> As soon as the priests who carried the ark reached the Jordan and their feet touched the water's edge, the water from upstream stopped flowing. It piled up in a heap a great distance away . . . while the water flowing down to the Sea of Arabah (that is, the Dead Sea) was completely cut off. So, the people crossed over opposite Jericho. The priests who carried

the ark of the covenant of the LORD stopped in the middle of the Jordan and stood on dry ground, while all Israel passed by until the whole nation had completed the crossing on dry ground. (Josh. 3:15–17)

The entire population of Israel crossed through on dry ground. This population was anything but small. We're talking in excess of 2.5 million people. Every last one of them walked across the sandy ground while the waters were stacked on either side.

This incident was clearly not an accident. It was a miracle of God. God effectively says to Joshua, "There's something I want you to do with this moment":

"Choose twelve men from among the people, one from each tribe, and tell them to take up twelve stones from the middle of the Jordan, from right where the priests are standing, and carry them over with you and put them down at the place where you stay tonight." (Josh. 4:2–3)

Why in the world would they have to carry stones from the middle of the Jordan and stack them up in their camp? Because God wanted them to have a physical reminder of the story He was writing. Joshua said to them,

"Go over before the ark of the LORD your God into the middle of the Jordan. Each of you is to take up a stone on his shoulder, according to the number of the tribes of the Israelites, to serve as a sign among you. In the future, when your children ask you, 'What do these stones mean?' tell them that the flow of the Jordan was cut off before the ark of the covenant of the LORD. When it crossed the Jordan, the waters of the Jordan were cut off. These stones are to be a memorial to the people of Israel forever." (vv. 5–7)

God essentially says, "Tell the story of what I did for you. Talk about how I delivered you. Share how I showed up. Describe what the water looked like—how miraculous it was! Pick up the stones, stack them up, and then have a conversation about what I did among you."

You see, in the Hebrew culture, remembering was not just a mental activity. Remembering was an action for them—remembering crossed their lips. The Hebrew word for "remember" is *zakar,* which means "to think about, meditate upon, pay attention to; remember, recollect; mention, declare, recite, proclaim, confess."[47] They *talked* about what happened. They were to proclaim what God had done among them—for them. They were to mention it, recollect it, recite it, *declare it.* This moment was to have significant impact not only on those who experienced it firsthand, but on the generations to come.

I can't imagine ever forgetting something so remarkable, so miraculous. Yet, they did. Israel forgot.

> They forgot what he had done,
>   the wonders he had shown them.
> He did miracles in the sight of their ancestors . . .
> He divided the sea and led them through;
>   he made the water stand up like a wall. . . .
> In spite of all this, they kept on sinning;
>   in spite of his wonders, they did not believe. (Ps. 78:11–13, 32)

They watched it happen and then they forgot. Somewhere along the way, they must have stopped telling the story. Maybe the stones felt old or too familiar. Maybe they just got tired of talking about it. Whatever the reason, they failed to recall the wonders the Lord had worked on their behalf, and as a result, they didn't remember the rescue they received.

So much of the time I think, "Well, really, Israel, how can you not remember something so remarkable? You guys are just dense!" Then the Holy Spirit gently whispers, "Laura, you're a bit like them, don't you think?"

True story. I am.

God reminds me of all the times He's shown up in my lifetime and made it clear that He is at work, only for me to forget. He's shown me His hand at work and

---

47. *Theological Wordbook of the Old Testament*, edited by R. Laird Harris, Gleason L. Archer Jr. and Bruce K. Waltke (Chicago: Moody, 1999), electronic ed., 241.

has done miraculous things in my life and I fail to remember. I start to think I'm going to have to make the next thing happen myself or it's going to have to be me who holds it all together.

We can't guarantee we will never forget because we're human. We will forget His works from time to time, but the more we keep talking through the things God has done in our history and sharing the ways He's shown up throughout our lifetime, the more apt we are not to forget. Remembering requires active participation. We have to be intentional—just like we have to be intentional about setting our minds and hearts on things above and fixing our eyes on Jesus.

Forgetting can lead to difficulties. For Israel, it led them away from God into sin. When we forget, it leads to stress, doubt, fear, confusion, anxiety, and ultimately to disobedience and sin. When we forget what God has done, we typically have forgotten who He is as well.

If we know these things about forgetting, why don't we choose to remember? It seems like a simple, logical choice, doesn't it? We know that remembering God's story in us will make us feel more secure. It won't secure prosperity or grant us perfect circumstances, but it can alleviate some of the stress, fear, doubt, confusion, and anxiety.

Remembering increases the peace we experience because we know who God is and we carry with us how He has shown up before. We can know that—come what may—He will redeem and restore our stories. *There is nothing that will ever happen to you or to me that God cannot redeem.* That's His nature. We've seen Him do it over and over again in the pages of Scripture and in the lives of His people.

Then what keeps us from remembering if we know these things to be true? For some of us, it's sheer pride. We've not recognized God's hand at work in our own stories. We live in the place God warned Israel about in Deuteronomy 6, thinking we built all we have with our own hands.

For some of us, it's just that we're moving too fast to be reflective. One of the greatest snares of the enemy is busyness. We are in a culture of productivity and progress. And progress slows down for no one. We are bound by the "tyranny of the urgent." Social media bombards us. Overcrowded schedules overwhelm us. The demands of our culture shout at us. Time seems to slip by and before we know it, we've forgotten the things that matter most, including our walk with Jesus.[48]

For others of us, there are some things we'd rather just forget. Maybe as you look at your story, there are things you might prefer to have never happened. Maybe they happened to you or in spite of you or because of you. Maybe you just wish you could erase that footage from your life film.

But you must know, there is no place or time or space in your history or in mine where God was not present. He has been right there with you all along (Ps. 139:7–12). He had a plan to redeem your story for His glory and renown too. The deepest darkest thing you did that was so terrible—the thing you don't want anyone to know about and you don't *want* to remember. *He was with you.*

What we usually end up remembering is what we did and how we messed up or how horrible the thing was that someone did to us. In those moments, our eyes are on us—our sin and our circumstances or the sins of others. *We need to fix our eyes on Jesus* (Heb. 12:2).

So, whose story are we actually telling? If I'm remembering and telling my own story of failure, my future probably won't look so great. But if I'm remembering and telling God's story of redemption, understanding God can redeem and restore *anything*, I can step into unfamiliar territory with more hope and greater confidence.

There are things we can do in our current culture to slow down enough to notice what God is doing and to remember—to proclaim and declare His story at work in us. The first is spending time in God's Word. We see His story play out in the pages of Scripture. When we see what God has done in His Word, it strengthens us now. He doesn't change. Those stories remind us of *who* God is—He is mighty

48. Robert L. Hubbard Jr., *NIV Application Commentary: Joshua* (Grand Rapids, MI: Zondervan, 2009), 168–69.

and powerful, compassionate and gracious. Knowing His story begins in reading His Word.

Another helpful practice is the Ignatian daily Examen. This guided prayer walks you through your day with simple questions: Where did I see God at work? Where did I see His love for me? Where did I say no to Him? Where do I need to repent and what do I need to confess? What am I stepping into tomorrow where I need to open my hands to Him?

Whenever I practice this prayer for a few days in a row, I'm always surprised by what I see. We focus on what we choose to focus on. If we don't intentionally choose to focus on anything, the tyranny of the urgent takes over. This tactic is a favorite of the enemy. If you forget God, and Satan can keep you in the place where stress, fear, and anxiety rule your life, he thinks he's won!

Except the enemy has not won at all.

Knowing his strategies helps us in the battle. He doesn't *want* us remembering God's story of redemption because he knows it will empower us to step forward with courage.

Talk about your story. When was the last time you shared a piece of it with someone else? When did you last take the time to speak out loud something God has done in your life? Sometimes it's hard to do. We don't have to share the whole story with every person because not everyone is capable of receiving it. But when it's right, share your story. When we share our stories, it strengthens the faith of those who hear what God has done as well as solidifying who God is in our own remembering.

At the same time, listen to the stories of others. Be a safe place for people to share their stories without judgment. Welcome the remembrance of others. It's a privilege to carry the weight of another person's story. When we speak our stories and when we listen to others, it transforms us, helping us to remember we did not build what we have, but it was God's hand at work.

Our own remembrances must be spoken and declared. They must be so engraved on our hearts that we cannot help but speak about them. May God engrave His story on our hearts. His story is definitely one worth telling.

REMEMBERING

Can you even imagine it? Walls of water surround you on every side as far as you can see. How can this be? Can you imagine all the fish and sea creatures swimming up to the water's edge just to catch a glimpse of the thousands of people traipsing across the dry, dusty ground at the bottom of the river? Amazing! Wouldn't you want to remember this moment forever? I wouldn't want to forget it either.

Today we're going to take some time to read through the centerpiece story for this week's journey, Joshua 3–4. Recognizing God's miraculous hand at work in the pages of Scripture helps us to see His hand at work around us in our everyday lives.

We're going to read this passage a couple of times, looking for the answers to the questions below during each reading. Take some time to imagine what the scene was like. Read these words as though you were a part of the caravan of Israelites making their way into the Promised Land.

Read through Joshua 3–4 slowly with these questions in mind. After reading, set aside the text for a moment.

Now begin to imagine the scene as if you were right in the middle of it. Answer the following questions:

What do you see?

What do you hear?

What do you smell?

What's your position?

Who else is there with you?

What are you feeling?

What's the mood of the crowd?

What is your response to all of this?

What questions do you have?

What fears do you have?

Don't worry about historical accuracy. Just allow God to bring the story to life. These people we read about in Scripture were real people who walked the earth and had feelings and thoughts much like ours.

Write down some of the things you are noticing from your responses.

Now read through Joshua 3–4 again.

Ask God to reveal to you what He wants you to see.

What are your observations about the text?

What is God calling you to do as a result of reading this passage?

Heavenly Father, You do miraculous things every day all around me. Open my eyes to see the works of Your hands in my life and the lives of those around me. I want to remember what You have done. You are all-powerful and are writing every single piece of my story. Thank You for that truth. Help me to believe it and live what I know is true. Amen.

My Prayer:

Journaling Prompt:

When have you had a "Jordan-parting" moment in your life that you don't want to forget? Write about that story in your journal today. Even if it seems insignificant, it matters to your story. Write the details of how God showed up and what He did. Thank Him for what He did. Consider finding a stone and writing on it the date the event occurred. Place the stone in a prominent place where you will see it often.

WEEK 6 | DAY 2

MEMORIAL STONES

We are wired for story. Stories draw us in. And what makes a story great isn't always a happy ending. A captivating story makes us laugh one moment and cry another, only to laugh again.

Our own stories are no different. At times, it's easy for us to move through the everyday parts of our lives without stopping to consider what our personal stories contain.

Your story matters.

Your story is captivating. It is filled with drama, like everyone else's, but the Author of your story has made it unique. There is no other story exactly like yours.

And that's why it matters.

It also matters that you remember it. Not just in your mind, but in the Hebrew sense of the word. Do you recall the Hebrew word for remember? It is *zakar*, which means "to think about, meditate upon, pay attention to; remember, recollect; mention, declare, recite, proclaim, confess."[49] We're not just to file our stories away in our minds, but we are to pay attention, to recount them, and mention them to others. We're to proclaim what God has done and recite it in conversations.

It's important to recognize where God has shown up in every chapter, at every plot twist. He writes the best stories. We just have to stop long enough to notice them.

Today may be just the beginning of a greater work for you. I invite you to step into it with courage. It may be easy. From my own experience, my guess is that it will be a bit difficult, but worth every hard moment.

---

49. *Theological Wordbook of the Old Testament*, edited by Harris, R. Laird, Gleason L. Archer Jr., and Bruce K. Waltke (Chicago: Moody, 1999), electronic ed., 241.

God instructed the Israelites to choose memorial stones (as on the cover of this book) or set up altars of remembrance throughout their history. He did this so they would talk about what He had done with the next generation. When we tell our stories, we remember what God has done for us, through us, and sometimes, in spite of us. He reminds us of who and whose we are. He demonstrates His relentless love in the ways He shows up over and over again.

Take some time to prayerfully write out your memorial stones today. What have been the most significant events in your life—filled with both joy and pain? Walk through the decades of your life and draw out your most important memorial stones. For each of these events, answer these questions:

Why was this significant?

What did I learn about God in this moment?

How was God with me in this moment?

How did this transform me and make me more like Christ?

Is there work I need to do to heal?

And, perhaps the most important question of all:

Was there a scriptural truth God etched on my heart in this season? What was it?

Remember, this very well may be the beginning of a bigger project. Working through your story takes time, so be kind to yourself. Ask God for patience in the process. Doing work like this also requires community. It takes others to help point out God's presence in the midst of the hard seasons. Ask others to point out where God was present. If needed, choose a trusted, faith-filled friend or a Christian counselor or spiritual director to help you find peace and healing.

Before you begin, read through these verses from Psalm 77. Let them be the background as you remember today. Write these words where you can see them as you work through your story. Pray before you begin, asking God to make these words evident in what He shows you today.

I will remember the deeds of the Lord;
    yes, I will remember your miracles of long ago.
I will consider all your works
    and meditate on all your mighty deeds.
Your ways, God, are holy.
    What god is as great as our God?
You are the God who performs miracles;
    you display your power among the peoples.
With your mighty arm you redeemed your people,
    the descendants of Jacob and Joseph. (vv. 11–15)

Begin writing your memorial stones below. Use additional paper if needed. Draw them out or write them. You could write them in your journal. Just begin. God's grace is sufficient. There will be nothing that will surprise Him. He's been there all along. Loving you anyway.

Almighty God, You are writing my story. You've been writing it all along. You have a plan for it and that plan is good. You've ordained all my days. You've done so out of love for me. Thank You for that truth. Help me to believe it and live what I know is true. Amen.

My Prayer:

Journaling Prompt:

What surprised you the most about writing down pieces of your story? What did you see? How did God show up? How will this change your ability to step into the unknown trusting God?

WORDS

Words are funny things. It's remarkable how much power something on a page possesses. It's even more remarkable how much power those same words carry when they are spoken out loud. Power to wound. Power to heal. Power to change things.

One of the biggest aids we have in remembering God is His Word. Having Scripture hidden in our hearts keeps our eyes fixed on what God has done. His Word reminds us of the promises and truths we tend to forget. It reiterates God's character, and sometimes we all need to be reminded of what He has done throughout history—how He's been faithful.

Many times in my life Scripture has calmed me or reminded me of a truth about who God is that I needed to remember desperately. One significant moment is when I went through severe physical pain accompanied by deep emotional grief. The ugly cry of the century shrouded that moment. The greatest comfort was a favorite passage of Scripture I had hidden in my heart. All I could do was repeat those words over and over.

I don't recall how many times I spoke them out loud, but peace came as I repeated these words. The pain didn't go away. The grief didn't disappear. But God reminded me of who He was right in the middle of the sorrow and pain. His peaceful presence came through the healing power of His Word.

There are many other Scriptures I have encountered that have helped me remember certain moments when God has taught me something in some way. I'm sure you have some too. Having a list to reference at times helps.

As we begin our encounter with words today, let's take some time to first write down some Scriptures that hold special significance to you and your story. Write them in the space below and list why they are important to you. If you don't have a list, go back through the earlier pages of this study and write the most significant Scriptures below. Answer these questions: When did you learn this truth? Was there a life event that taught you this truth?

As we've seen this week already, remembering is vital. It changes our perspective about our current situation. It reminds us of God's consistent character. After all, if He's shown up before, He'll do it again. Remembering grows our faith and fosters hope deep within us. Who doesn't need a little more of that?

Over and over again, God commands His people to remember and to not forget. God has worked miracles and done deeds that you may not have taken the time to fully consider. I know that's true for my own life. God shows up unnoticed all too often.

Read through our memory verse for this week:

> I will remember the deeds of the Lord;
>   yes, I will remember your miracles of long ago.
> I will consider all your works
>   and meditate on all your mighty deeds.
> (Ps. 77:11–12)

Take a look at the dictionary definition of the word *consider*:

Consider: to think carefully about, especially in order to make a decision; contemplate, reflect on; to think, believe, or suppose; to pay attention to; regard.[50]

This definition makes me realize I don't really spend much time "considering" all God's works in my life. I want to learn how to reflect on and pay attention to how He has worked, is working, and will work on my behalf all around me throughout time.

One of my favorite truths about God is the many facets of His character. I love to dwell with the different, powerful names of God. Many of those names have significant meaning in my journey along the way. He is my Healer, my Redeemer, my Restorer, my King, my Abba Father—and so much more. These aren't just words. They show who God is.

Each of these words means a great deal to me, and when I hear them, I can think of specific things God has done in my past in order to teach me about His character. I need to be reminded because if I don't choose to remember, I forget easily. I want to live in a way that constantly considers what God has done in my life. I want to remember where God has shown up and shown who He is.

Take a look at the list of the names of God below. If there are other names of God or characteristics not listed here you resonate with, write them down as well.

ALMIGHTY GOD	**ETERNAL GOD**	**THE LIVING GOD**
PROVIDER	**MY BANNER**	**HEALER**
RIGHTEOUSNESS	**PEACE**	**HOLY ONE**
KING	**JUDGE**	**SAVIOR**
REDEEMER	**ABBA FATHER**	**HUSBAND**
ROCK	**SHEPHERD**	**ANCIENT OF DAYS**

50. Consider. Dictionary.com. *Dictionary.com Unabridged*. http://www.dictionary.com/browse/consider?s=t.

Which ones resonate with you? Why?

Are there events in your past that connect to the names you chose?

Are there names of God you would add to the list? What are they and why are they significant to you?

Lord Jesus, thank You for the power of Your Word. It changes me. Your Word is a lamp unto my feet and a light unto my path (Ps. 119:105). I want to remember You well. Remind me how each of these names has become evident to me as You've carried me. Your Word is powerful. Your name is powerful. Thank You for those truths. Help me to believe them and live what I know is true. Amen.

My Prayer:

Journaling Prompt:

Write out one of the Scriptures you chose today. What is the significance of this Scripture? Is it tied to a piece of your story? Write down the connection. Which name of God is most significant to you? Why is this so? Which names of God do you struggle with? Why do you think you struggle with those names? Which characteristic or name of God do you need most right now? Why?

WEEK 6 | DAY 4

FORGETTING TO REMEMBER

When was the last time you forgot something you were really supposed to remember? Sometimes what we forget doesn't really matter all that much. Other times, we forget and it leads to spoiled food in the sink (like when a person forgets she laid out meat to thaw for dinner—I cannot confirm or deny I know anything about that). Or we forget and it leads to our child not having the primary ingredients for that project they have to turn in tomorrow at school (again, not that I would know).

Other times we forget and it leads to us losing a bit of our perspective regarding the nature and character of God. We forget what He's done and we lose sight of who He really is.

Forgetting has a long history. We are not the only ones who forget what God has done. Israel has a history of forgetting too.

Today's reading is a long text, but an important one. In Psalm 78, the author walks through the reasons we want to remember as well as what happens when we forget. Take some time with this text today.

Read through Psalm 78:9–39, paying special attention to the verses emphasized.

> The men of Ephraim, though armed with bows,
>   turned back on the day of battle;
> they did not keep God's covenant
>   and refused to live by his law.
> THEY FORGOT WHAT HE HAD DONE,
>   THE WONDERS HE HAD SHOWN THEM.
> He did miracles in the sight of their ancestors
>   in the land of Egypt, in the region of Zoan.

He divided the sea and led them through;
    he made the water stand up like a wall.
He guided them with the cloud by day
    and with light from the fire all night.
He split the rocks in the wilderness
    and gave them water as abundant as the seas;
he brought streams out of a rocky crag
    and made water flow down like rivers.

But they continued to sin against him,
    rebelling in the wilderness against the Most High.
They willfully put God to the test
    by demanding the food they craved.
They spoke against God;
    they said, "Can God really
    spread a table in the wilderness?
True, he struck the rock,
    and water gushed out,
    streams flowed abundantly,
but can he also give us bread?
    Can he supply meat for his people?"
When the Lord heard them, he was furious;
    his fire broke out against Jacob,
    and his wrath rose against Israel,
for they did not believe in God
    or trust in his deliverance.
YET HE GAVE A COMMAND TO THE SKIES ABOVE
    AND OPENED THE DOORS OF THE HEAVENS;
HE RAINED DOWN MANNA FOR THE PEOPLE TO EAT,
    HE GAVE THEM THE GRAIN OF HEAVEN.
Human beings ate the bread of angels;
    he sent them all the food they could eat.
He let loose the east wind from the heavens
    and by his power made the south wind blow.

He rained meat down on them like dust,
 birds like sand on the seashore.
He made them come down inside their camp,
 all around their tents.
They ate till they were gorged—
 he had given them what they craved.
But before they turned from what they craved,
 even while the food was still in their mouths,
God's anger rose against them;
 he put to death the sturdiest among them,
 cutting down the young men of Israel.
IN SPITE OF ALL THIS, THEY KEPT ON SINNING;
 IN SPITE OF HIS WONDERS, THEY DID NOT BELIEVE.
So he ended their days in futility
 and their years in terror.
Whenever God slew them, they would seek him;
 they eagerly turned to him again.
They remembered that God was their Rock,
 that God Most High was their Redeemer.
But then they would flatter him with their mouths,
 lying to him with their tongues;
their hearts were not loyal to him,
 they were not faithful to his covenant.
YET HE WAS MERCIFUL;
 HE FORGAVE THEIR INIQUITIES
 AND DID NOT DESTROY THEM.
TIME AFTER TIME HE RESTRAINED HIS ANGER
 AND DID NOT STIR UP HIS FULL WRATH.
He remembered that they were but flesh,
 a passing breeze that does not return.

Israel encountered God in the desert—He continually provided for them miraculously, but they forgot. Once He met their need, they moved on. When they were satisfied, they forgot what He had done—how He had worked among them and defied the laws of nature on their behalf.

But God was gracious again and again. He was merciful, sparing their lives. He forgave their sins and continued to do the miraculous on their behalf. At times I just can't imagine how they could see God move in such unbelievable ways and forget Him.

Then, God gently reminds me I do the same thing. He delivers me only for me to forget. I forget what He's done. I forget who He is. I overlook His promises.

Oh, how I want to learn to remember!

How have you forgotten the miracles God has done in your life?

How has forgetting affected your walk with God?

How has it affected how you face your unknown future?

Why is it important for us to talk about the things the Lord has done?

What do those conversations do for your faith?

How has God continually shown you grace and mercy in spite of your forgetfulness?

Most Holy God, Your grace amazes me. I am forgetful. You are merciful. I long to remember what You've done—both in my own life and throughout time. You do not change. Thank You for that truth. Help me to believe it and live what I know is true. Amen.

My Prayer:

Take a moment today to write a prayer of remembrance and thanksgiving for the miraculous acts God has performed in your life that you do not want to forget. What do you want to remember? How can you tell of His wonderful acts? How can you pass the memory of these saving acts on to the generations to come? Write your prayer below:

Journaling Prompt:

Take some time today to write out a part of your story in greater detail. When was a time you felt the presence of God—either in loss or in joy? How did God show up in this moment? What changed in you as a result? Write to remember. Then, be courageous and share your story with someone you trust.

WEEK 6 | DAY 5

LOOKING BACK

Over the last six weeks we've covered a lot of ground! We've learned God has made Himself known (Acts 17:24–28). We've been honest about our anxiety and the downward spiral. We've discovered the different Greek words for knowledge and have seen how those apply to our relationship with God.

We've listened to Jesus ask us, like the disciples, if we believe our fears instead of Him. We've compared scarcity and abundance, discussing how the differences impact our everyday lives. We've examined what kind of cornerstone Jesus actually is in our lives. We've dug into the extraordinary story of Jehoshaphat and saw how his worship affected Judah's victory.

We've looked at the reality of pain in our lives—how circumstances affect the way we view the future. We've seen how God is with us in every situation. He stays. Even when it's hard.

Last, we've encountered the power of remembering and what it truly means to remember.

That's a lot. If you're like me, in this moment, you'll finish up the study, set it on a shelf, and move on to something else. But I think God longs for real, lasting transformation in you and me. Real transformation takes time. Effort. Marinating. More time. Reflection and, most important, action.

It's so easy for me to miss the things God really wants to do in me. Sometimes I get bogged down with information. Other times I'm just moving at a speed that's so fast I can't possibly hear or see what God wants for me. Still other times I just want change to happen right away, but it's going to take a bit more patience and time for me to see the transformation.

Today, take time to gather your other notes and your journal. Pray and ask God to reveal to you one truth He wants you to walk away with, making a lasting change, for each week of the study. Ask yourself, "What Scriptures resonated with me the most this week? What were the greatest insights—the *aha* moments? What invitation is God extending to me right now as a result of what I'm learning?"

Take some time to linger in what you've learned. To remember.

WEEK 1: A KNOWN GOD

What Scriptures resonated with me the most this week?

What were the greatest insights—the *aha* moments?

What invitation is God extending to me right now as a result of what I learned this week?

WEEK 2: WHAT DO YOU *REALLY* BELIEVE?

What Scriptures resonated with me the most this week?

What were the greatest insights—the *aha* moments?

What invitation is God extending to me right now as a result of what I learned this week?

WEEK 3: CORNERSTONE

What Scriptures resonated with me the most this week?

What were the greatest insights—the *aha* moments?

What invitation is God extending to me right now as a result of what I learned this week?

WEEK 4: OUR EYES ARE ON YOU

What Scriptures resonated with me the most this week?

What were the greatest insights—the *aha* moments?

What invitation is God extending to me right now as a result of what I learned this week?

WEEK 5: REGARDLESS, YOU ARE GOOD

What Scriptures resonated with me the most this week?

What were the greatest insights—the *aha* moments?

What invitation is God extending to me right now as a result of what I learned this week?

WEEK 6: I WILL REMEMBER

What Scriptures resonated with me the most this week?

What were the greatest insights—the *aha* moments?

What invitation is God extending to me right now as a result of what I learned this week?

PRAYER FOR THE DAY

Lord Jesus, You have shown me so much. I know I will never arrive where You want until I meet You face to face. Give me the courage to step into the invitations You are extending to me. Your grace is enough for me as I move toward You. You love me as I am but call me to something greater because of that love. Thank You for that truth. Help me to believe it and live what I know is true. Amen.

My Prayer:

Journaling Prompt:

What are your thoughts as you see the insights you've gained over the last six weeks? Where have you already seen growth and change? What do you desire to do with your new knowledge? What will keep you moving forward? How can you step into the unknown in a different way than when you began? What does your "This I Know" list look like now?

WEEK SIX: REFLECT AND ACT

Well, here we are. The last reflect and act day of the study.

I wish we could sit down over a cup of tea (okay, you can have coffee, if you'd like). I'd love to hear your story. I'd love to hear what God has done in you through these few weeks too. My words can't change anyone. I know that for sure. The Holy Spirit is the One who holds the power to transform. He's been at work in you these last six weeks. I would love to hear how you've seen Him work, how He's spoken to you through His Word:

mystory@lauradingman.com

In this last reflection and action day, take some time to first reflect on what you wrote in your Day 5 study summary as well as new truths you encountered in this week's material.

Take some time to answer each of these questions in your journal:

What new truths did God reveal through my time in His Word this week?

What challenged me?

What am I still struggling to believe?

What are God's invitations to me right now?

Are there themes or patterns in what God is showing me? If so, what are they?

What action steps do I need to follow as a result of what I've learned this week?

I pray you know how incredibly loved you are by our amazing God. I pray you have a deep sense of peace as you see how God has written and continues to write your story. I pray you can surrender to Him and trust Him for what comes next. He holds it all. And He won't let go. Ever.

Lord, give me I pray:

A remembering heart for the things that have happened
An attentive heart to what I have heard
A forgiving heart for what has hurt
A grateful heart for what has blessed
A brave heart for what may be required
An open heart to all that may come
A trusting heart to go forth with You
A loving heart for You and all Your creation
A longing heart for the reconciliation of all things.

A willing heart to say "Yes" to what You will.[51]

—Leighton Ford

---

51. From Kurt Bjorklund, *Prayers for Today: A Yearlong Journey of Devotional Prayer* (Chicago: Moody, 2011), 33.

CONCLUSION

INTO THE UNKNOWN

Over the last six weeks, your unknown future has probably not become any clearer. You probably haven't found a working DeLorean either! I do hope, though, you have discovered more about the God who goes before you into the future you cannot see.

God has made Himself known.

He walks with us, allowing us to truly *know* Him (*epignosis*),
not just *about* Him (*gnosis*).

Our Jesus commands the winds and the waves.

He is greater than any fear we face.

We can trust Him with everything that lies before us.

He is our great cornerstone, laying an unshakable foundation.

The Holy Spirit dwells *with* us. We are never alone in whatever we may face.

Our future is still unknown. It always will be. You may still have great fears about what lies ahead for you. Remember that courage isn't the absence of fear, but moving forward even in the face of fear. My hope for you is that maybe you have a little less fear knowing what you now know.

So, what *do* you know? As you make a new list of the things you know about God, I pray it looks a bit different now than when we began. I pray you are believing different things about who God is and are living as though they are true. I don't know what lies ahead for you, but what I do know is, the God who is for you goes ahead. He sees it all and knows just what you need.

God is writing a remarkable story in you. Some of it is yet to be seen. Even if it holds heartache, He will write it for good. He always does. It's remarkable because He's weaving it into the story of heaven. Your story is God's story. Don't forget that.

Laura

MY DEEPEST GRATITUDE—

To My Church Family at The Creek—You make three dimensional what Christ meant the church to look like. I cannot imagine doing life anywhere else. Thank you for consistently challenging me to grow and change and simultaneously loving me where I am. Thank you especially to the Worship and Creative Arts Team. You all are my family. You help me remember who God is. And I love you all the more for it.

To Sibyl—You have taught me to stare into the unknown without fear. You have helped me access the peace of God in real time. I am so grateful.

To Judy—You have believed in a girl who barely believed in herself as a writer. Thank you for the amazing ways you encourage me to bring my best for the kingdom. Thank you for seeing potential in this work in its most raw form and helping to breathe life into it. You are a gift. I'm deeply grateful to not only share kingdom visions, but to call you friend.

To the "Tribe Crazy Train"—You girls ground me. In the anxiety and chaos, you make me laugh. You bring calm to my crazy. Thank you for being anchored in Jesus. Your God stories grow my faith. I wouldn't want to step into the unseen future without you all locking shields with me. I'm grateful I don't have to.

To My Prayer Warriors—Your prayers have literally prayed this into being. I know you will keep praying for everyone who reads the words printed in this book and you will mean every word from the depths of your hearts. You are my lifeline. You have carried me to the throne and that is a gift I cannot repay. I'm so grateful for your love and prayers.

To Paulette—I'm so glad you asked me so many years ago if I wanted to write a Bible study. I thought you were crazy. I suppose we both still are. Thank you for seeing something in me that I didn't even know was there. I treasure your friendship and your deep love of God's Word.

To Lise—Thank you for sending me an email at 4 a.m. telling me I was a writer. I didn't believe it, but your words ushered in a new curiosity God grew. Your encouragement and friendship through the years have shaped who I am.

To Sandra, Wendi, and Alisa—You girls have taught me the true meaning of grace. Thank you for loving me as I am, but loving me enough to not allow me to stay that way. Thank you for providing space for laughter through this process.

To Mom and Dad—You have always taught me to trust Jesus not just by your words, but by the way you live. We faced a lot of unknowns in my childhood that I never even knew. Your faith in God was lived out loud. Thank you for the groundwork you laid.

To Abigail—I pray daily for your unknown future, knowing God holds it in His hands. You are helping me to let go and trust God more fully every day. I love you bigger than the world.

To Matt—I don't know what our future holds, but I'm grateful I get to walk into it next to you. Thank you for holding my hand in the hard times and for pointing me consistently back to Jesus. You are the best part of my story. I love you.

To Jesus—Thank You for the constant You are. You have saved me and I am grateful. You are enough. Always. My heart and my future are Yours.

Bible Studies for Women

IN-DEPTH. CHRIST-CENTERED. REAL IMPACT.

I AM FOUND
978-0-8024-1468-7

AN UNEXPLAINABLE LIFE
978-0-8024-1473-1

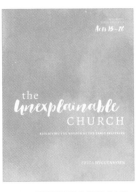

THE UNEXPLAINABLE CHURCH
978-0-8024-1742-8

HIS LAST WORDS
978-0-8024-1467-0

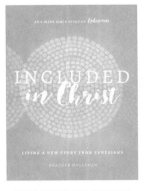

INCLUDED IN CHRIST
978-0-8024-1591-2

WHO DO YOU SAY THAT I AM?
978-0-8024-1550-9

HE IS ENOUGH
978-0-8024-1686-5

MOODY
Publishers®
From the Word to Life®

Explore all our Bible studies at
moodypublisherswomen.com

ALSO AVAILABLE AS EBOOKS

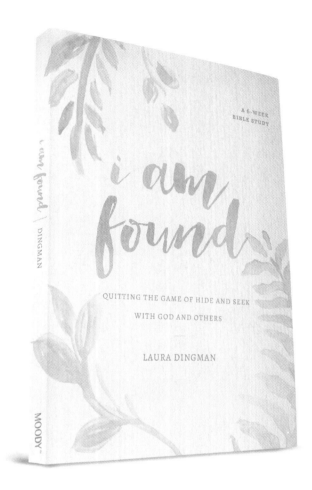

MOODY
Publishers®

From the Word **to Life**®

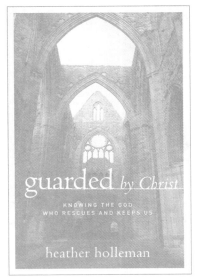

978-0-8024-1487-8

Guarded by Christ: Knowing the God Who Rescues and Keeps Us

Heather Holleman

We all need maturity in Christ that prepares us not just to endure anything, but to live from the strength and peace of Jesus in every season. *Guarded by Christ* helps women cultivate this maturity, reconnecting them with the Savior who rescues, keeps, and holds us with His love.

ALSO AVAILABLE AS AN EBOOK

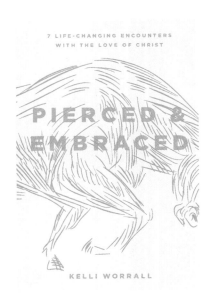

978-0-8024-1631-5

Pierced & Embraced: 7 Life-Changing Encounters with the Love of Christ

Kelli Worrall

Pierced and Embraced digs deeply into seven encounters that Jesus had with a wide variety of women in the Gospels to show how His love can be equally transformative in our lives today. It mixes attentive Scriptural engagement with personal narrative and relevant application, making the content fresh, accessible, engaging, and practical.

ALSO AVAILABLE AS AN EBOOK